The Secret War of
CHARLES FRASER-SMITH

Books by Charles Fraser-Smith

The Secret War of Charles Fraser-Smith.	(£3.50. p & p 80p)
Men of Faith in World War II.	(£2.50. p & p 80p)
Four Thousand Year War.	(£3.20. p & p 80p)
The Man Who was 'Q' (by David Porter)	(£3.95. p & p 80p)

Obtainable from:

MRS. M. S. FRASER-SMITH
LITTLE COMPASS
1 WESTGATE
LOUTH
LINCOLNSHIRE
LN11 9YN

The most complete collection of secret gadgets in Britain, as described in Charles Fraser-Smith's books, is on display at Bickleigh Castle, Nr. Tiverton, Devon. Open Easter to end of May – Wednesdays, Sundays and Bank Holidays. June to mid-October daily (except Saturdays) 2 to 5 p.m. Parties by arrangement. Telephone: 0884 855363. Also at Dover Castle, Dover, Kent. Open Daily, closed 24–26 December and 1st January.

The Secret War of CHARLES FRASER-SMITH

The 'Q' Gadget Wizard of World War Two

With
Gerald McKnight and Sandy Lesberg

Published by:
M. S. FRASER-SMITH

First published in Great Britain by
Michael Joseph Limited,
27 Wrights Lane,
London W8 5TZ.

This edition published by permission by M. S. Fraser-Smith, Little Compass, 1 Westgate, Louth, Lincolnshire. LN11 9YN.

British Library Cataloguing in Publication Data

Fraser-Smith, Charles
The Secret War of Charles Fraser-Smith
1. World War, 1939–45 ——— secret service
2. World War, 1939–45 ——— personal narrative
I. Title
II. McKnight, Gerald
III. Lesberg, Sandy
940.54′86′41 0924 D 810.S7

ISBN 0 9528408 0 4

Typeset by Saildean Limited, Surrey and
Printed in Great Britain for M. S. Fraser-Smith,
by Cox & Wyman Ltd., Reading.

CONTENTS

ILLUSTRATIONS

1

GUNS FOR LOVE

THE DAY BEFORE leaving Room 39, University College Hospital, Gower Street, I said to my night nurse, Miss Compton, 'Two things I shall remember about my nights here – you, and a harder pillow than I ever had in the war.' This was early in 1946. She gave me a sharp look. 'Thanks for the compliment,' she replied. 'Only one thing I'll remember you by – that man in the Scriptures who was "stiff necked and disobedient".'

I smiled, knowing that she had no notion of how close she had come to the truth. My piece of the war had been, I suppose, more unorthodox than that of almost anyone alive. I had seen the whole show from an oblique point of view, supplying equipment and gadgets to secret agents in the field or to POWs trying to escape. Because I had worked completely underground, using as a 'cover' the innocent-seeming guise of a temporary civil servant in the Clothing Department of the Ministry of Supply, my methods had certainly been individual. In most cases I had been forced to go well outside 'normal channels' to get anything done at all. And knowing when something of mine went well – a gadget that really worked and out-foxed the enemy, perhaps helping save a valuable life – had been all I needed by way of inspiration.

As the Bible says: 'No one shall enter (the Kingdom of Heaven) who maketh lies.' That had been my job. I had used every possible form of deception to beat the Germans, employing many of Britain's largest and finest firms under conditions of absolute secrecy to do so. In the First World War, warships disguised as freighters and unarmed trawlers had been known as 'Q ships'. My gadgets were much the same: 'Q gadgets'.

Before Miss Compton left me I gave her this parting shot: 'I hope I'll see you up above. I'm quite sure you'll be there, but I'm not so sure about myself.'

'That doesn't depend on you,' she said. But she was unaware of my day to day occupation during the years of all-out warfare. As she administered my 'dope' for the last time, she gave a quick extra jab of the needle. I asked what on earth that was for. 'That's for love,' she told me.

In its own particular way, my very secret war had been waged for the same reason. For the love of those who were fighting and dying while I was at home in comparative safety.

I know the debt they owe to the many fine firms and individuals who answered my call on their time and skills to perfect the secret and cunningly devised gadgets I was ordered to make – often at the shortest possible notice – for the various secret service departments I worked for. For the love of all these people and their associates alone I should wish my story to be told.

Indeed, had my lips not been sealed by the Official Secrets Act – binding me to absolute silence for thirty years – I should have paid tribute to these courageous and unselfish people years ago. At the end of the war I was able only to drop them a personal, guarded note of gratitude and leave it at that. Public acknowledgement of this curious, unstinting 'Q Force' has had to wait until now.

So, too, have my tremendous debts to the men and women who were the active users of my products. How those men and women, dropped by parachute or landed from submarines behind enemy lines, viewed my armoury of gadgets I can only guess from the few scraps of feed-back which came my way, often by merest chance. How much or little our shot-down aircrews evading capture, or escaping prisoners of war, depended on the secret equipment with which I and others provided them is equally unknown to me. But my deep respect for them, for all agents and serving officers and men who faced the terrors of pursuit, can now be paid; as it can to the underground saboteurs and resistance workers of many nations whom we also helped to supply.

Would I have managed to overcome Civil Service inertia if I had not stretched myself – and the rules – to the limit? Take that evening in 1943, at the war's height, when my office telephone rang and a voice I knew, giving a code name I immediately identified with the secret department classified as M.I.6 (responsible for espionage abroad), sounded in my ear. How else could I have coped with that?

The message was brief. Three hundred miniature automatic pistols were needed, urgently. For the French maquis, or Britain's agents of the cloak-and-dagger Special Operations Executive (S.O.E.), I surmised. But my job was to supply, not to ask questions. All I was told was that no less a number would suffice, even though both my caller and I knew that no handguns of any description were available, other than those earmarked for front-line service.

I looked at my watch, realising (with a sinking of spirits to which I was well accustomed) that I had barely thirty minutes to catch one of the few remaining trains running through the London blitz to take me home to Rickmansworth and my one good meal of the day – usually Brussels sprouts, or some other fresh vegetable from my garden. The tone of my caller, Commander Ridley, underlined the fact that, if nothing else, this order had to be carried out immediately. The deadline was only three weeks ahead.

I put down the telephone and waited until my secretary, who knew nothing of my secret role, had left for the night. Then I pondered the problem. All fire-arms had to be surrendered by private individuals in wartime Britain, under Defence of the Realm regulations amounting to martial law – and carrying the same Draconian penalties. Hence it was extremely unlikely that any dealer in small arms would possess a supply suitable to my needs. Also, there was not the slightest possibility of getting the things manufactured in the time. What was left?

Automatics are small flat weapons (unlike the bulky revolver) which can easily be hidden on the person or kept in position under the armpit by a strap. And many servicemen and others returning from active service abroad had, I knew, brought small German and Italian models with them as souvenirs. Though technically contrary to the law, an official blind eye was customarily turned towards such irregularities. Even so, how was I to get hold of these trophies?

No earthly use sifting through my list of London and provincial gunsmiths, of that I was certain, having tapped them dry during the previous months with increasingly thin results. I made a desperate appeal by telephone to the section of Military Intelligence which carried a stock of the much larger 42s. But, as I expected, they had nothing my size at all.

Next contact was the Small Arms Section of the Ministry of Supply. Here I received a definite 'no.' None were being manufactured in the country and none would be shipped from the United States for several months.

Third contact was the Firearms Department of Scotland Yard. They said, 'Nothing doing.' They had advertised and circularised owners to surrender or sell their small firearms since the beginning of the war, and during the last months none had come in at all. I said I had personally received one of these notices for my own automatic. (This was a Belgian gun I had smuggled out of French Morocco, when France collapsed. While a quick 'run down' of my clothes was being made, I had lifted it out of my trouser pocket hidden in my handkerchief and pretended to blow my nose.) I also said that the pre-war price offered was too low for today's market, and the very patriotic people they had drawn on were now exhausted. Could they not re-advertise, offering half as much again on the pre-war price?

This, they said, they could not possibly do without consulting the Home Office. Furthermore, they thought there would not be very much hope of success, and it would take some days or weeks to alter the present ruling. I asked if there would be any objection to my going ahead and advertising for the guns myself? They thought it would be 'unwise'. I had better consult the Home Office, they said, on account of some rather strict regulations which nobody seemed to understand fully. Obviously, nothing further could be done that evening.

Next morning at 9.05 I rang an important Home Office official. He had not arrived and I was told he would not be coming in until at least 10.15 since he had 'worked late the previous evening'. This meant an hour's delay, and a quick initial step-off is essential on such a job. I realised that my V.I.P. might not even be in at 10.15, and that fixing an appointment with him could take several hours, even a day or two. After which I would most probably be handed a file, or files, of regulations to go through; and then if the official agreed to my proposals, the whole matter would have to go to a higher level still.

The appalling prospect of having to deal with this kind of bureaucracy began to depress me. Then I thought what it would mean if I had to let my Military Intelligence contact down. It made me jump up from my seat; and, as it so often does, inspiration came with action. The time had come, I told myself, to use my official position in a way which no other Civil Servant would have dreamed of doing. The Home Office official's late arrival was partially to blame: he had shown me that unorthodoxy simply had to be applied if we were to win the war. Or so I reasoned, without the least idea of the trouble I was letting myself in for.

I had realised that if I stuck to the rules there would be little prospect of obtaining the guns inside three months, let alone three weeks. I needed a go-ahead man, one who was not too *au fait* (any more than I was) with the various Home Office regulations. And I'd hit on the ideal chap in my mind – an American who was London manager of a well-known British firearms firm in the Midlands. Slovak was his name, and fortunately he was on the spot when I telephoned to say that I'd be round to see him in ten minutes. I ordered a car from the Ministry car pool.

Now, my way of dealing with outside firms and individuals was always the same. Initially, I pretended to be a powerful member of the Ministry of Supply. Only when I was satisfied that the director, manager, or expert I was talking to was able to carry out the secret work I was actually seeking would I reveal the truth. And then only when I had obtained their signature to the Official Secrets Act, binding them to absolute silence on pain of being thrown into the dungeons of the Tower of London at the very least! Never once was I let down, or betrayed, so far as I know.

This time I was dealing not only with an outsider but with a foreigner, as well. But since the United States was our greatest ally, that was all right. When Slovak had taken the oath of secrecy, I told him what I wanted. His face fell. He had not seen so many automatics at one time for years. I explained: my theory was that they *did* exist, but that a better price was needed to winkle them out. Would he advertise for me – and try and bring them in? He agreed at once.

I scribbled a 'contract' for Mr. Slovak for 300 automatics on Ministry of Supply note-paper without even asking how he would be wording his advertisement. Then I left him to his own devices. I had only asked him to make it clear that good prices would be paid, according to the condition of the weapons. And on no account was he to advertise in the London area, but to concentrate on the large coastal cities and towns, such as Southampton, Plymouth, Liverpool, etc. I feared that advertisements in London publications would be spotted by Scotland Yard; I presumed they would be too busy to sift through provincial ad pages. I also guessed that local constabularies would be less knowledgeable about this sort of thing, and therefore inclined to accept the advertisements as nothing unusual. (It turned out that I was right with one important exception. But more of that later.)

Slovak certainly lived up to the American reputation for hustle. Every editor bowed before his tornado-like entreaties. He did not even have to appeal to me to apply Ministry 'pressure' on any awkward newspaper to get immediate insertion, in spite of their limited advertising space being fully booked for weeks ahead. Within eight days he was sending round to my office regular batches of two or three dozen automatics. Some of the weapons were of superb workmanship. One weapon was silver-plated; another had solid gold mountings, and the German chromium-plated guns were perfection. I soon realised that much of what I was being offered was battle-field loot!

The money asked by the owners ranged from pre-war prices to anything up to 80 per cent above. Many asked even higher prices and I promptly returned these weapons. One man had the audacity to ask five times the pre-war price, so I informed the owner (as his 'obedient servant,' of course, since I was writing on official, M.O.S. notepaper), that the price he was asking was more than the black-market price in Belgium under German occupation.

But what a good sight to see the guns rolling into the office. In sixteen days we had some 240 of them, all serviceable. And I still had five days left in which to complete the target. So all, I thought, was proceeding according to plan. But that was when I fell foul of the law.

Coming into the office on the seventeenth morning, my secretary informed me that Scotland Yard wanted me urgently. By this time I had taken her completely into my confidence, which was just as well. She proved an invaluable ally. So I picked up my black briefcase, and on the way out asked her to ring Scotland Yard and *insist* on knowing why they wanted me. Of course, if it was of a secret nature and could not be revealed over the phone, I told her I would understand. But she was *not* to let them know I had already been in unless they cornered her (I did not want to get involved with deliberate lies but I had recalled what a businessman once said to me that 'Civil Servants do not lie, they're master craftsmen at avoiding the truth'). 'Avoiding tactics' was to be my maxim for the next few days.

Twenty minutes later I telephoned my secretary-accomplice from a phone box. She had neatly extracted the information with no complications. Apparently a police officer on the south coast had seen the advertisement for firearms and thought it might be irregular. Scotland Yard, however, had become quite rattled, and I was requested to go to them at once and explain why I had allowed my American man's firm to get involved in such an activity.

This was becoming too much of a good thing. It meant more thinking, more improvising, and I felt this job had had its full quota of such deviousness already. Ordinarily, I could have asked my M.I.6 master, Commander Ridley, to square things for me without any trouble. But this time I had overstepped the mark by acting on my own. I decided I'd better lie low, at least until we'd completed the task. Any harm the advertisement might have done, such as letting the enemy know we were short of these weapons, was now done and could not be rectified. The great need was to hold off any official inquiry until the last sixty automatics were in.

I therefore told my secretary I would not be in the office but was out on a special call. I hoped I would not be too long. She dutifully rang up Scotland Yard and informed them of the message she had received, saying she could do nothing further but would get me to ring directly I came into the office, or inform me of their message if I rang in to her. Naturally I avoided ringing up the office for any such contact. I did ring Military Intelligence H.Q. at two o'clock and checked that no fresh job had been assigned to me.

Having covered myself as best I could, I felt I would be safer in the country in case Scotland Yard tried to contact me directly. So I took a day off and went for a long walk. Next day I contrived to arrive at the office rather late. Scotland Yard was contacted. They started rattling 600 rounds a minute at me and finished by saying that the Home Office Security Department was going to handle the case. Would I give them a ring? I had my wits about me sufficiently to realise that this would mean further delay, so I welcomed it. Twenty-six hours had already been gained, and the automatics were still trickling into the office.

When I eventually contacted the Home Office, it was by delayed action. I was overwhelmed on the telephone by an irate official who was plainly all set to tear me off an almighty strip. Eventually I managed to squeak, 'Look, I'm awfully sorry to be the cause of all this, but it's too much for me to grasp over the 'phone. As I have to go out *now* on an urgent job, would you oblige me by dropping me a line about it all? I promise to attend to the matter directly it arrives.' I felt this would give him at least a couple of hours' work, as well as another two hours getting it over to me, but he fell for it and agreed to my suggestion – before immediately regretting his decision. I could almost hear his brain-waves crackling and a deep breath being drawn as he tried to reverse his stand. While he was still making up his mind I snapped down the receiver. And before he had time to ring me back, rushed out of the office.

On phoning some hours later, my helpful secretary informed me that a special messenger had brought a large and important looking envelope from the Home Office. I later found it consisted of three pages of closely-typed foolscap. The points made were excellent, and perfectly applicable. The letter instructed me to retract the advertisements immediately. I accordingly wrote to the firm and had my letter delivered by special messenger. There were now only a dozen more pistols needed, and I knew that Slovak would have these in hand in the time remaining before the retractions could take effect. So I breathed freely. The job had been done. Only the Home Office letter remained unanswered.

I went home, put a wet towel round my head, and eventually glimpsed a possible way out. Obviously Slovak, as a completely innocent party to my scheme, had to be fully exonerated. He had merely – and most effectively – acted on my instructions. Since he was American (and I was only a *temporary* government official, of short duration) we could plead ignorance of the official regulations. I wrote an impassioned plea, claiming total innocence and stressing the fact that I had acted as I had only after an urgent and difficult demand from Military Intelligence.

I heard nothing for a week, then a phone call came: would I come and see a certain high official. At our interview, he asked me why I had been attempting to gather in such a large quantity of small firearms by irregular means, instead of contacting the appropriate branch of the Ministry of Supply? I explained that one of my first contacts had been to the department and they had turned it down flat. He then said, rather stiffly, that arrangements had been made for this department in future to handle all such requirements. Would I therefore introduce my Military Intelligence contact to the head of this M.O.S. Department forthwith (and, in so many words, keep my unorthodox fingers out of their well-ordered official pies). I did so on the following day in the happy knowledge that I had bucked the system, helped the war effort, and (if only just) held on to my job.

Thus ended the battle – for so I regard it, although it has had to remain a reward unto itself until now, since nobody could share its secrets. Where the automatics went to, how many later turned up in the hands of French or other resistance movements during the recovery of Europe from the Nazis, all that is, and always will be, unknown to me.

It was not until after the war that I found out how Ridley had obtained ammunition for the guns. None was available in Britain. Apparently he passed the word to an American liaison officer in their equivalent of M.I.6. This man persuaded the mayor of Chicago to broadcast an appeal to the city's gangsters. It produced an immediate response, and ammunition galore. Even a few dozen small automatics came rolling in. Ridley, in gratitude, sent me some special Rimfire Long Rifle Hollow Point rounds for my own automatic.

I had to wait ten years for the final chapter to this little episode. I'd been asked to go to Holland with another chap who, like myself, was a farmer; we were collaborating on an article for a farming periodical. We chatted on the voyage about our wartime activities, though my vow of secrecy forbade more than a reference to 'Ministry of Supply' on my part. My companion looked up when I mentioned it.

'That's funny,' he said, 'I once gave one of your chaps a pretty hard time while I was in the police. I believe he came close to being cashiered.'

Suspicion dawned. 'Where might that have been?' I asked innocently.

'Oh, Portsmouth,' he said. 'I happened to be Chief of

Police there at the time. He was making some sort of killing in firearms, I believe. Anyway, we got on to him.'

I grinned. 'And did you ever hear who it was you so nearly cashiered?'

'No,' he said. 'But I don't expect he'd take it too hard. In fact, I think it all came right in the end, if I recollect correctly.'

I held out my hand. 'Absolutely right,' I said. 'It did. And I'd like you to meet him in person.'

I've often thought since how pleasant it would have been had all my projects ended like that. Not that it was such an outstanding coincidence to meet wartime contacts, especially from the Intelligence sections, on post-war farms. Many of us drifted towards the land. So did many others. In my case it was where I had come from; I was returning to my roots.

2

FIRST STEPS

I HAVE ALWAYS had an inquiring mind and a decidedly independent spirit. Going with the stream, at least without good reason to do so, has not been my way. This doesn't mean that I broke laws and rules made for the common good; not at all. I believe firmly that discipline is one of the most profitable aspects of life. There can be little true freedom, peace, or happiness in family or national life without it. Yet my aim from a very early age has been to explore all sides of every issue, and rarely to accept anything handed to me.

Perhaps because of this I have led a very varied life, from farming in Morocco where I managed extensive farmlands for the Moroccan royal family and chief religious judge, as well as owning two farms of my own, to running an orphanage in Tangier and starting another on my farm outside Marrakesh. When war broke out I was thirty-six and ready for anything.

My family and I got away from Casablanca in a Norwegian freighter carrying phosphates and, after being twice bombed at sea, arrived in England seventeen days later.

I spent the first weeks despatch riding in London where the Blitz was beginning in earnest, and then started a job at the Avro aircraft factory at Yeadon. My wife and son stayed nearby with her family in Leeds. It was there that one Sunday evening I was asked to talk at a service of the Open Brethren Evangelical Church, of which I had been a member since the age of seventeen. The talk I gave was more of a lecture than a sermon. I described my pioneering missionary work in Morocco and the often unorthodox methods I had used to keep my various projects alive. G. Ritchie Rice, the director of the Ministry of Supply in Leeds, was one of those listening, and he had brought along Sir George Oliver, then Director General of the M.O.S. in London.

Ritchie Rice, as I was to learn later, was a kind, warm-hearted man who had – and has still, in his nineties – a quiet humour and an ever-beaming expression about his round face. He was then in his mid-fifties and had been involved in several missionary society committees. I think he was impressed to hear how a man like myself had used initiative and a certain elasticity of mind to work with the Arabs. He must have felt that it displayed an inventive character, one which could operate independently and without specific guidelines. Both he and Oliver chatted with me at the end of the evening.

The next day I was asked by Rice if I would visit him at the Ministry headquarters in Leeds. After a searching talk, mainly about my past activities, he asked me exactly what I was doing at the moment. I told him merely marking time, kicking my heels at Avro until something more challenging came along. He then mentioned a man named E. D. Alston who was working for M.O.S. He was apparently an expert in clothing and textiles, but was about to become involved in a rather special, highly-secret operation. Rice gave me no details. Alston, he said, would need an assistant: would I be interested?

The conversation so far had been informal, even casual. Yet I sensed that this was a serious and exciting offer and I jumped at it. Within the following week Rice had arranged for me to leave Avro and report to M.O.S.

in Leeds. For the first three weeks – no doubt while my record and personal history were being minutely checked by Security – I only handled matters to do with clothing and textiles. Then, with no explanation given, I was sent for and requested to sign the Official Secrets Act. It imposed on me thirty years of total silence regarding all my work from that time forward – yet I still had no idea what that work would be. I was simply told that I was no longer to be concerned with what I had been doing, and was to report immediately to head office in London. (Alston remained in Leeds as my opposite number, but this I only discovered later.)

So began what I now look back on as a wartime role of Alice in Wonderland proportions. With my wife and small son, Brian, I moved down to my family home in Croxley Green, outside Rickmansworth, in Hertfordshire. From there I could commute to London daily, as did many other wartime civil servants. The Ministry of Supply had requisitioned Portland House in Tothill Street, Westminster, from the Portland Cement Company, and this was where I was to base my operations.

The office given to me was on the first floor, just along the hallway from Ritchie Rice who had also moved down from Leeds. We were adjacent to various directors of the Ministry. My room was not at all grand, as befitted a very junior (temporary) civil servant. I suppose it was about twenty feet by twelve, with a large dark-oak desk and – most important of all – three telephones. One was local, one long distance, and one – the red one – priority. My personal assistant-cum-secretary moved in with me and I had her telephone connected up with all of mine, so that she could listen to everything being said and avoid repetition. She was thus able to carry on with routine projects, leaving me to pursue the heavy work.

Since I was primarily a farmer, I had never done much filing. Also, I had gathered by now, the fewer records I kept the better. My job with the Ministry was merely a pretence, a 'cover' to shield far less innocent activities. It was very cleverly thought out, because a minor official from the Clothing section of the wartime Ministry of Supply could go anywhere and call on anyone, to carry out his official instructions. And without giving away his or their purposes.

Actually, as became even clearer as my first 'orders' reached me – from such awe-inspiring departments as 'M.I.6' and 'M.I.9' (top-secret Intelligence departments which many in the country at that time had never even heard of) – I was their floating production and procurement man. My job was to supply material on demand for highly secret and often sensitive projects on behalf of nearly all Britain's Intelligence services. Others did similar work in different fields (Major Clayton Hutton at Beaconsfield, for one), but so far as I know I was the only civilian not assigned to a particular service.

I was never specifically told what I should and should not put my hand to. The orders simply came in, chiefly by phone, and I did my utmost to fill them as quickly and quietly as possible. Looking back, I'd say that fifty per cent were direct orders from Intelligence sections which knew exactly what they wanted. They simply used me as a provider, somebody who could get on to the firms who made such things and ensure that they would deliver on time and under conditions of absolute secrecy.

Another forty per cent went to departments which knew only roughly what was required. They left me to figure out the precise means by which their orders could be obtained. The remaining ten per cent came out of my own head, developed and presented to the appropriate agency whenever I sensed a need. These, of course, gave me the maximum satisfaction; I knew that I had managed to inject a small but apparently useful cog into the war machine.

The way I received my instructions was also ingenious. People I never, in many cases, saw face-to-face throughout the entire war – and do not know to this day, other than by their code names – would ring me on one or other of my telephones. With my P.A. listening in on the extension I would pick up and listen. A voice would ask: 'C.T.6?' When I replied in the affirmative, the voice would identify itself by a code name and, in as few words as were necessary, give me the requirement. Each department would employ a different code name in its dealings with me. Though this could have been confusing, in practice I developed a sixth sense about it. Where there was any doubt, or a difficulty which could not be explained fully over the telephone, we would set up a meeting.

These usually occurred over a cup of coffee in a café near my office. As far as humanly possible I dissuaded all contacts from coming to see me. Even Ritchie Rice, I later learnt, knew almost nothing of the full scope and nature of my most secret work. I kept as low a profile as possible.

In the case of suppliers, those firms and individuals with whom I placed my orders, I made it a rule to visit them, rather than vice-versa. Because petrol was severely rationed, I used to work out careful plans for each journey in advance, getting in as many calls as possible en route. On an average morning I might go to six different places. An official car and driver, which I was entitled to commission from any one of the secret Intelligence departments I served, would take me on my rounds. But, though I had regular contact with these car pools, and with the departments themselves by telephone and occasional outside meetings, I invariably kept away from their offices. Especially those of M.I.6 and S.O.E., both for my own as well as their protection. I had no wish to be connected with them in any way, and used our own M.O.S. car pool whenever possible.

There was another snag involved in using Intelligence section cars, particularly those of S.O.E. One never knew who, or what, the drivers might be. On one of the rare occasions when I did resort to this department, my lady driver turned out to be a Belgian agent who was having to lie low in London for a bit. Her driving, as we shot up Whitehall and round Trafalgar Square, made me think I was back in Paris.

Remembering all the names of the secret departments presented something of a headache at first. And, of course, when the United States Intelligence departments joined our own, I had my work cut out. Somehow one managed. Before long, I had completely mastered the British list; M.I. was Military Intelligence; D.M.I., its director. M.I.2 and 3 were both concerned with interpreting intercepted enemy reports, while M.I.5 handled our internal security services. M.I.6 was my most intimate contact and our major secret Intelligence service abroad (the equivalent of America's C.I.A.). Our Secret Service chief, whom Ian Fleming in his James Bond novels calls 'M', was in fact known as 'C'. M.I.8 dealt with codes, signals and such-like, including the captured German 'Enigma' and 'Ultra' code-machines, which were so invaluable to our forces in reading enemy signals. (In one case, a battle order of Rommel's reached us even before he got it himself!) M.I.9, from which I received many instructions, was responsible for interrogating enemy prisoners of war, and for providing escape techniques for our own prisoners, as well as methods for shot-down airmen to evade capture. M.I.14 was a similar set-up to M.I.8, but exclusively for Germany and German-occupied Europe. And there was S.O.E. (Special Operations Executive) formed during the war to recruit, train and operate agents and resistance forces behind enemy lines.

Others (which I had at least to be able to recognise) included Ian Fleming's own department of Naval Intelligence, N.I.D.; the department's director, D.N.I., and the B.C.R.A. (Bureau Central de Renseignement et d'Action) of the Free French wartime Intelligence and Sabotage Department.

However, it was not every day that we heard from more than a few of them. When one of our more habitual callers came on I could usually tell the moment I heard their voice in my ear. Early training on a farm in winter, when one had to listen for the cries of a sheep or lamb buried in snow, had made my hearing acute.

When M.I.9 came on, for instance, I instantly knew that it was them when the disembodied voice announced 'M.I.S.'. That was their call sign. Equally 'BRO' heralded M.I.6. It stood for Broadway, and their headquarters in Minimax House next door. We seldom heard from M.I.5, since they were concerned with internal security only. But S.O.E., after they became active, were regular callers, and in their case I *always* recognised the voice.

I still have no idea who some of the voices belonged to. Or what their role was. Ask me who was the highest-ranking person I met, or spoke to, during the entire war and I could not possibly tell you. Presumably it was somebody in the War Cabinet, but I've no idea who. Secrecy, as I soon learnt, depended on ignorance. The less anyone knew the better.

3

NIGHT AT THE OPERA

I USED OVER 300 firms in and around London for the delicate, and often extremely difficult task of producing my secret gadgets and equipment. Some knew they were being employed in a clandestine 'Q factor' campaign; others did not. For the most part they performed magnificently.

My task was to communicate to these firms the extreme urgency and need for what I asked from them. It had earlier been suggested that I should wear the uniform of a major to lend added authority. I decided against it. Any influence I might have with these people, I believed, would more readily come from my own way of approaching them than any badge of official rank.

In any case I was aware that the sight of military uniform could only make my suppliers less enthusiastic (given the military reputation for unbusinesslike behaviour). A civil servant, I believed, was more likely to be treated with respect, provided he knew what he was talking about.

Also, as a Ministry of Supply official, I was able to obtain raw materials in short supply, which gave me considerable leverage. Mostly, I relied on my technique of being as brief as possible in all my personal dealings. I said my piece, did my business, and got out.

It seemed to me quite unnecessary to allow anyone I had dealings with the opportunity to size up my role too keenly. The first principle of any Intelligence work is that the smallest possible number of people should gain an overall picture of it. Each cog must be kept separate and apart from the whole machinery. I therefore let my suppliers feel that anything I asked them to do for me was complete in itself. If they ever suspected that there were others being used on the same operation, they were wise enough not to say so. By casting my net wide, I gave my real purpose away as little as possible.

For the same reason, the men and women on the other side of my strange sphere – the Intelligence department contacts whom I supplied – were equally cautious in their relations with me. We worked in isolation. My impressions of them were therefore rather sketchy.

Soon after World War Two began, the head of M.I.6 was Col. Stewart Menzies, formerly of the Life Guards. He ruled behind a padded door, seated behind a big antique desk reputed to have belonged to Nelson. He took on Claude Dansey as his deputy.

The chief's office was on the fourth floor of 54 Broadway. It was an old and most uninteresting construction, just opposite St. James Park underground station. This was my station too. My office in Portland House was practically adjacent. Broadway had nothing to distinguish it from any other drab office building. It was, in fact, superb cover, with the old plate of Minimax Ltd., the fire extinguisher manufacturer, who had previously occupied the premises, still fixed to the wall outside.

I believe they had to work on a shoe string, though one would have thought that such vital departments of secret Intelligence would be provided with all the finance needed. That was not Britain's way.

I only went into Broadway a couple of times, and then only for something extremely important which I didn't dare mention over the phone. Otherwise, my contact was through a Scottish girl who worked alongside Commander

Ridley and Commander Rhodes. She had a delightful telephone voice.

Ridley and Rhodes were my chief M.I.6 contacts. Both were Naval men, though I had no idea who they really were – or their exact status – until much later. Commander Philip W. Rhodes, R.N. died shortly after the war. He was the M.I.6 Naval Intelligence liaison officer with M.I.9 at Beaconsfield – liaison between N.I.D./M.I.6/M.I.9. He had been taken prisoner after the Battle of Jutland so he knew all about P.O.W. life from the inside. I never met him in person; he was simply a voice on the telephone. I did meet Ridley, though after doing so I'm not sure I knew him any better. We went to an opera together one night when I was fire-watching for incendiary bombs. I'd mentioned the duty to him while talking on the phone earlier that day and he'd said, 'Oh, I'm up this evening too.' 'Well,' I suggested, 'why not let's break the monotony and take in a show?' He agreed right away.

This was quite a common practice among fire-watchers in our department. One always had five minutes or so warning, and provided your base knew where you were, and you had a car standing by to rush you back in an air raid, it was understood that a bit of light relief was a good idea.

At Ridley's suggestion we went to see *Madam Butterfly*. I don't think I'd ever bothered to go to an opera before in my life. But Ridley was keen. He liked opera, he told me. That was about all he did tell me. He was a thinnish, balding man with an upright, Naval carriage, but I had no way of knowing his true rank (we were both wearing civilian clothes) or indeed whether or not he had been in the Navy at all. At various times I heard him referred to as 'Captain', at others as 'Commander'.

I found it strangely awkward to be with him. For some reason it seemed oddly wrong to be with this secret man, as if our relationship was in some way destined to remain at arm's length – a clandestine, cloak-and-dagger affair of clipped telephonic exchanges and coded identities, as though anything more intimate was breaking the rules. Perhaps in the strictest sense it was, certainly he never repeated the process. We did not meet again during the war, or after it, in spite of our joint activities.

4

SHOTS IN THE DARK-ROOM

My first assignment, while still at Leeds with Alston, had been to produce 100 Spanish army uniforms out of thin air. In 1940 there was a very real threat of Spain entering the war on Germany's side. If that had happened we should have needed to infiltrate S.O.E. agents immediately by whatever means possible, and an army disguise in that militaristic country would have been as good as any other.

I began with the cloth. A sample uniform was provided, and I sent a small piece of its material to one of our leading textile firms with an order to produce the amount I wanted in exactly the same drab shade and poor quality. I even specified in my order that the fabric should be 'thick, coarse, cheap and nasty.' I might as well have been talking to the moon.

My chosen manufacturer, a canny Yorkshireman, presumably scratched his head, reckoned the Ministry of Supply were simply being excessively patriotic and careful with the country's spending money, then decided it was time to make his own contribution to the war effort. He sent me a sample but in a much finer cloth, and with a note saying that I wasn't to bother my head about the extra cost, as that would be 'absorbed on Britain's behalf'.

The generous manufacturer promptly had his nice cloth returned to him with a note stressing the need for what I'd asked for in the first place. He still refused to believe I was being anything but stiff-necked and 'civil service' about the whole thing. He sent me another sample almost as good. It took three goes before I got what I wanted, and no doubt I left him wondering why we had treated his act of generosity so shabbily.

It was the Spanish scare, however, which taught me another lesson about procuring oddities in wartime. Never try to pretend that things are normal when they are not. I needed Spanish matches and anti-mosquito cream to go with the uniforms; these were simple enough. But I also had to include flea and lice powder, and this was another story. Some of the workers at Keatings famous firm producing this useful insecticide in Britain became suspicious that British servicemen were being subjected to lousy quarters. A newspaper reporter telephoned the Ministry, where fortunately he was put on to somebody who knew nothing at all about it, and was laughed to scorn. But it was a near thing.

All this, of course, was before I signed the Official Secrets Act. I was not yet in a position to bind my suppliers to secrecy, and to put the true case, or some essential parts of it, to them. Later on, this is what I did most religiously. As soon as I found myself in touch with a supplier who could and would provide what I was after, I immediately made him swear and sign the oath, after which he became my willing accomplice. In a good many cases I found that directors of the larger British firms were, in fact, already engaged on secret war work, and had signed the Act beforehand.

Another event arose out of my clever idea – or so I thought at the outset – to provide our prospective Spanish agents with garlic-laden breath. In a nation as garlic ridden as the Spanish I had recognised that easy detection of a foreigner could follow any lack of this smelly substance. To overcome the necessity of having to educate our people in its somewhat exotic taste, I therefore decided to flavour chocolate with it. I included this in their equipment. The trouble was that I had to persuade honest English chocolate manufacturers that I was not pulling their legs – and without explaining my reasons.

From all these early problems I learned how to get the best out of the many suppliers I later had to deal with; the more than 300 firms listed in the small notebook which was my sole dossier of activities, and which I have still.

But if the problems with a few firms were sometimes a headache, they were nothing to the difficulties which cropped up internally. From time to time I found myself in the middle of most bothersome inter-service squabbles. These made me even more glad than usual that I was a civilian, even in my peculiar role.

Often, these petty disputes and inter-departmental bickerings occurred for no good reason that I could see. In the European theatre Bomber Command, for example, took a very dim view of the work of the S.O.E., whose agents were hourly risking their necks behind enemy lines. That famous war hero 'Bomber' Harris phoned me one day in a distinctly critical frame of mind. Harris obviously had no time for the S.O.E. which he derided as amateurish and irresponsible, and wouldn't approach them himself, but he needed their help.

The aerial photos he was getting after his air raids, he said, simply weren't good enough. They failed to assess the whole story. Could I rig up some smallish cameras and let some of 'those S.O.E. chaps' have a crack at photographing some of his target areas? And would I mind awfully putting all this to the S.O.E. people on his behalf.

In other words he not only wanted me to come up with the smallish cameras, suitably camouflaged so they could be transported in and out of occupied Europe, but would I also recruit the S.O.E. for him, since Bomber Command wouldn't reach beneath itself actually to make the arrangements?

The most effective miniature camera at that time was the Minox, and I knew right away that I would have my work cut out to find enough of them. They were in extremely short supply. It was either a matter of finding a quantity already manufactured and in good working order, or of having to go flat-out to reconstruct a batch of our own. Which is why I saw this immediately as a top-priority job. The Minox was made in Lithuania, and it was a fair bet that the Germans had been maintaining production for their own purposes. However, I managed to come up with an initial three or four, and the Board of Trade promised to give me a line on any Minoxes brought into and sold in this country.

Then I sat down and stared long and hard at the wall of my office, my normal way of seeking inspiration when in a tight spot. Who, among the leading camera specialists in Britain, could come to my aid? The name Wallace Heaton floated into my mind as if by divine inspiration (which I don't doubt it was), and without further ado I picked up my red telephone. I have never made a more satisfactory call in my life.

Old Wallace must have been in his late sixties or early seventies when I contacted him. He responded with the vigour and zeal of a two-year-old. Having begun life in Liverpool, where he rose to the ownership of a good-sized pharmaceutical business by the age of twenty-five, he had then become fascinated by photography. It had brought him to London and his well-known premises, where I was invited to go and see him, at 119 Bond Street, smack in the heart of the fashionable world of clothing, cosmetics and highly-priced antiques. In no time at all, he had made photography quite respectable.

This was the wise, bright and extremely affable old man who greeted me with a warm handshake – large, like everything about him – on my arrival in an official car a few minutes later. He had recently retired, I gathered, as managing director to leave the day-to-day running of the business to his son John, or Jack, as he entreated me to call him. Wallace was now chairman of the company, but still very much the presiding genius. I felt an immediate surge of confidence as we talked over my project. It didn't depress me in the least that both father and son's offices were poky little places, hardly big enough to swing a cat in. Or that our interview took place with Wallace sitting at the desk and Jack and I leaning on door-posts.

I, of course, told him nothing of the secret purpose of my visit. I merely asked if he could find any means of acquiring, for the Ministry of Supply, as many Minoxes as possible. He said nothing until he had examined my official, and by now travel worn, pass. Then he nodded his big head and said cheerfully: 'Shouldn't be too difficult.'

If I noticed a slight twinkle in his eye, I said nothing. No doubt Wallace, too, had secrets he was not about to reveal. His intimate knowledge of all sorts of intricate camera processes must surely have been put to valuable use by our various Intelligence departments, quite apart from my own approach. But in secret warfare it is always possible for two people working for the same side, on the same mission even, to be left in total ignorance of each other's role.

After the war, I was told of a pretty Scottish girl whose war service had been in the signals branch of the F.A.N.Y. She had kept in round-the-clock contact with a certain agent in Italy, whose code name was 'Capitano John'. Then he had disappeared. When war ended, as she was sailing home on a troopship, she met and fell in love with a young officer. Months later, when they were married, he revealed himself as the very man with whom she had been in constant communication by secret radio. Often, she'd sent him little 'cheer up' messages of her own without the least knowledge of who or what he was, or any hope that they would ever meet. Yet her first reaction when her husband revealed his identity was that he was breaking his 'cover' – so strong was the habit of secrecy. Only then did she allow herself the enormous relief that 'Capitano John', her personal agent, was still alive. She had feared the worst, knowing that the average life of an agent in enemy territory was no more than three weeks.

I never knew whether or not the Heatons were involved in aerial reconnaisance or technical work of that sort or not, but they should have been. They were as resourceful and enthusiastic as any people I dealt with in the war. Wallace had a nice place down in Sussex and his son John took some baby pictures of my daughter there. They both found time to be friendly and cheerful in the middle of doing a good war job.

Because Wallace Heaton had been a founding member of the Photographic Dealers Association, and later its president, he was ideal for my purpose. It was relatively simple for him to enlist the help of all principal camera dealers in and around London. He sent out an urgent request to them to find every available Minox camera and buy it up. They really went on the hunt; advertising, telephoning old and new clients, the lot. I saw to it that they offered good prices, too.

The value of the Minox was in its small size and accuracy. The film was about one-sixth the size of a postage stamp and could shoot fifty pictures on a roll. Now that the Heatons were working, along with other dealers, to buy up whatever supply remained available in and around London, my next step was to investigate the possibility of manufacturing them ourselves.

It seemed out of the question to arrange anything sensible about the situation in Lithuania. We could, of course, kidnap the manufacturing foreman or design expert. But if he proved uncooperative it would be pointless having him hanging about in England, eating our prison food and taking up good space. So who could make them?

In discussing the problem with the Heatons they suggested I contact the people who make Dinky toys, the Lines Brothers.

Old Wallace's point, and it was a shrewd one, was that they were a firm with precision tools for making everything in miniature. I gathered, without going into it, that they had already been used to produce a number of important pieces of miniaturised equipment for the war effort. I arranged to see one of their senior directors.

He was helpful. If I left a camera with him, he said, he would have it broken down into its various parts and complete a fast costing of the job of manufacturing. I was delighted when he telephoned me only a few days later with the result, but not so happy when I heard his report.

Apparently the Minox possessed sixty-five different parts in all, and the initial cost of setting up the necessary jigs for manufacture would be, even in those days and with our help at the supply end, somewhere in the region of a £100,000. It was too much, even without the added wage bill for the highly skilled craftsmen who would have to be diverted from other war work to handle the job. There the story might have ended had not a most extraordinary piece of luck come my way.

It was a single phone call. The caller was completely unknown to me, which made it all the more mysterious since my numbers were not only unlisted, but under the strictest possible wraps of top-secrecy. How he obtained it I still have not the foggiest notion.

I thought at first he'd got a wrong number. That did happen occasionally, even on our secret lines, and normally one could get out of that situation without difficulty. But this time I was left in no doubt about the call being for me, however strange and unexpected. His voice – English, and not uneducated, but with no particularly identifiable accent – simply asked: 'Fraser-Smith?' I admitted it. Then the conversation went like this:

UNKNOWN CALLER: I understand you are on the search for a quantity of Minox cameras.
CFS: Who's this, please?
UC: There's an American chap who has a bundle of them. He is about to dispatch them to the U.S.A. for sale at a rather large profit, you see.
CFS: Who is this, please?
UC: It's not for the war effort at all, you know. Strictly for personal gain. (Pause) He has sixty of them.
CFS: Sixty? (I was stunned)
UC: Precisely. They can be found at ...
CFS: (Writing furiously) I really can't thank you enough – it's all most helpful. Won't you tell me now who you are?
UC: No, thank you. (Click).

I immediately got on to Scotland Yard who went round and collected my sixty golden cameras, confiscating them after the Board of Trade had determined that they were the subjects of some very intense war-profiteering.

With the several dozen already unearthed by the Heatons, the new additions filled the bill nicely and, with the supply of cameras now assured, my S.O.E. contact quickly agreed to carry out Bomber Command's request.

The next task was to find the best way to conceal the cameras. Cigarette lighters were the obvious place; one simply walked along until reaching the target then, as one lit a cigarette, a quick squint through the view-finder, an extra press of the finger and the picture was taken.

As to the pictures which my Minoxes produced, these, taken on the ground at great hazard by the S.O.E., showed extensive damage to many important German installations. When Hamburg was knocked about, nearly nine square miles were laid waste with a damage estimate of 77 per cent. Photographs appeared in a London newspaper over the caption, 'These official pictures, taken at ground level, come from a source which the Air Ministry cannot divulge.' S.O.E. was the source, and my Minoxes were in their hands.

Indeed, the little cameras played many vital roles, some involving harrowing experiences in the field. Michel Hollard, a French underground leader, was one of their chief users. Once he heard that a camouflaged naval dock was under construction at Marseilles. He found out it was underneath a large shipping warehouse. Disguising himself as a workman he got into the structure as the shifts were changing. Then, during the day, he snapped photographs of the installation – again using my Minox. The film reached London via Switzerland.

Hollard also kept hearing of strange new German installations under construction east of Dieppe. He went there to investigate. To get into the area, he loaded a suitcase full of religious literature and Bibles. The local office gave him a permit to do social work, ostensibly to help improve the morale of the labour force. It was a cunning cover.

Hollard found a workman who agreed to swap jobs with him for a sum of money. He began working at the installation, and soon discovered that it was designed to launch a very hush-hush, small, pilotless, flying-bomb to be aimed directly at London. In three weeks he had found similar installations under construction all along the coast.

His photographs of these flying bomb sites were secreted in a specially-made shaving brush which was another of my secret 'Q' items. They were quickly passed on to London. Guided by these ground level photos and supplemented by aerial photography, over 100 sites were soon demolished in the area, and London was spared for several months the devastation later inflicted by this most terrifying of all weapons.

Hollard's subsequent personal story came to me long after the war. He was finally captured by the Gestapo. After a year in a concentration camp, he was loaded and locked into the hold of a German ship. This was one of those crammed with 'unwanted' prisoners which were later abandoned in the North Sea with engines running but no crews aboard. When challenged by Allied aircraft or ships, the floating coffins would fail to heave to, thus inviting certain attack and destruction. This diabolical way of getting rid of helpless prisoners was typical of the Nazi mind, and horribly successful. Two of the ships, the *Deutschland* and the *Caparcona*, were sunk and thousands perished.

Fortunately Hollard was on the third, the *Thilbeok*. Locked in the hold, he heard the ship's engines started up and guessed the fate in store for them. Later that day he raised his voice, inviting all his doomed companions to link hands and pray. It is a matter of record that those prayers were answered. A Swedish Red Cross boat mercifully arrived at that moment and took possession of the hapless *Thilbeok*.

Yet all the good work of the S.O.E. and men like Hollard with the Minox on the ground would have come to nothing without a foolproof system of getting the film back to London. But how? I was instructed to find a way.

Two items were in constant use and would not raise German suspicions, I concluded. One was a torch and the other a shaving brush. Both afforded excellent hiding-places, while appearing to be quite innocent. A torch contains two batteries, and we replaced one with an empty watertight container into which the film was inserted. It looked like a genuine battery, but the one real battery provided all the power needed to operate the torch.

The shaving brush was a different story, and somewhat more complicated. We began by eliminating the usual commercial glue used to hold the bristles. Instead, we used a specially concocted, extra-strength, plastic cement that not only held the bristles in place but afforded a firm base. This could be screwed into a handle which had been skilfully hollowed out.

To prevent an ultra-suspicious German from unscrewing the top, no matter how tightly screwed on, I decided (with little more than a firm faith in the unswerving logic of the German mind) that since most objects that came apart unscrewed in anti-clockwise, right-handed manner, we ought to use left-hand threads. Anyone picking up the shaving brush and playing with it to determine if it was indeed subversive would merely tighten the top of the secret compartment.

The Kodak company then came up with an interesting bit of history. I had gone to see them about obtaining film for the Minox; not only were they quite willing to help all they could but they revealed considerable experience in the art of secret military photography. When I pressed them for details they showed me a camera about the size of a matchbox that excited me quite a bit, until they added that it could only take one picture at a time and that it actually had been used in the Siege of Paris by the French when the capital was surrounded by the Prussians during the Franco-Prussian War. Apparently in that action troop movements had been recorded from balloons hanging over the battlefields. The minute photographic plates had then been forwarded to London by carrier-pigeons, where the photographs were projected on a screen by a 'magic lantern'.

It was fascinating to learn that 'Q' gadgets had been successfully put to use in nineteenth century warfare.

Not all my experiences involving cameras went so easily. Ridley, my opera-loving M.I.6 contact, involved me in a chase for a Leica which almost led to my arrest. The message reached me in the usual way from Broadway: a curt telephone request. Ridley was not explicit, he simply told me he had to have a Leica in working order as quickly as possible. I gathered that it was to be passed on to a certain agent currently in London. I promptly dropped everything else and rushed round to a perfectly respectable dealer I knew who specialised in these things. He had one for which he wanted £300, and in view of the urgency I did not hesitate, but signed him an order for it on the spot. Then I had the camera wrapped and sent round to Ridley by special messenger, imagining the job to be concluded. Not a bit of it.

A week later two C.I.D. men came into my office. They said that the camera I had signed for and bought had just been sold for cash. My respectable dealer had rung them saying that a sickly-looking young man had brought the camera in to him. The serial number was identical to the one he had sold to me. Naturally, he had become suspicious and rung Scotland Yard. My C.I.D. visitors wanted an explanation.

I immediately produced my receipt, and surrendered the name and address of the recipient of the camera (exactly as a civil servant of the Ministry of Supply was expected to do). They went off with it a shade grudgingly as if I had robbed them of their prey. Perhaps I had. Their inquiries showed that the agent who had received the camera had had to go off quickly to another job; so he had casually put the camera in a drawer. Unfortunately, only a few days later, his son had been released from hospital after treatment for shell shock. Seeing the camera, and thinking it was useless whilst the war lasted (films were practically unobtainable) and needing some immediate money, he had taken it out and sold it.

The camera was duly retrieved from the dealer and returned to the agent, who probably got a rocket from M.I.6 for being so careless. My only concern was that he should not have lacked the equipment necessary to carry out his dangerous mission, whatever it may have been. I did get a hint later on from Ridley that it had, in the end, been satisfactorily carried out. That was my reward for a rather tiresome episode.

5

MODELS AND MASKELYNE

PHOTOGRAPHIC INTELLIGENCE and the model-making that grew out of it were called upon more and more as the war went on. For my suppliers and I, it presented a far bigger and more complicated undertaking than anything attempted before. M.I.6 included a little known but most vital area of planning, the model-making sections (M.M.S.). These worked closely with the Photographic Interpretation Unit (P.I.U.) and the Photographic Reconnaisance Unit (P.R.U.). And we supplied all the wood and other materials for these models, which is how I became privy to some of their most difficult projects.

The P.I.U. had taken over a large mansion between Marlow and Henley, near the little Thamesside village of Medmenham. In the eighteenth century this had been the headquarters of the notorious 'Hell Fire Club' at Medmenham Abbey, where an unhealthy group of atheists dabbled in so-called 'black magic.' Their sessions were held in the greatest secrecy and considered quite sinister. However, in World War Two a healthier form of secrecy took over!

The P.R.U. supplied P.I.U. with photographs taken from all angles of special areas, designated for bombing or ground attack, and the staff was called on to build scale models from these 'shots'. A good example was the magnificent Bruneval raid. P.R.U. and P.I.U. had discovered, from photographs, that a new type of radar station had been installed at Cap d'Antifer, in northern France. This was a headland, about twenty kilometres north of Le Havre and near a little village called Bruneval. It was essential that we obtained a close look at the installation.

Medmenham's most secret department now came into action – and fired orders at me. I had previously supplied special stereoscopic equipment to the P.I.U., and that was what I thought they were after when they came on the phone. But not so. They were screaming for models to translate the photographs into three-dimensional replicas. Once I had found them the materials, a bevy of their sculptors and artists with whirring fret-saws, hammers and special plastics quickly created exact miniatures of the whole area.

Cliffs and all contours were built to scale, fences, bushes, even ditches were included, so that the troops carrying out the raid could know exactly what they would encounter. Aircrews, paratroopers and commandos studied the model with infinite care. On the night of February 27, 1942, Bruneval was attacked by a small raiding-party who knew exactly what they were doing. The essential parts of the installation were dismantled on the spot and successfully brought back by sea.

The Würzburg, as the radar was known, had been erected on top of a 400 foot cliff, though fortunately a slope, 500 yards away, led down to a small beach. On old coastal maps of France it was called *'Descente des Anglais'* indicating that in the past it had probably been used by English armed forces. It was certainly used effectively in this raid.

S.O.E. had had to be called in here for detailed information about local German troops, and minefields, especially at the beach. Our French agents, 'Remy' (Gilbert Renault) and 'Pol' (Roger Dumont) had done a first class job. They'd obtained details of all the German guard movements and found that the small beach was *not* mined.

The guards were dealt with by paratroopers. Then technicians dismantled the vital parts of the radar and the

Navy evacuated the raiders and their booty. It was the model which guided them down the *Descente des Anglais.* We lost only two men, and six who were taken prisoner. But the Germans lost five killed, and one prisoner – a vital operator of the Würzburg who was brought safely back for interrogation.

For the landings in North Africa, aerial photography was organised from Gibraltar and Malta, but it was at Medmenham, using my materials, that the brilliantly achieved pictures were turned into models and topographical reports. Precise details of ports, airfields, defences, the exact width and condition of roads, the positions of pylons and telephone installations – all these were essential for successful, swift and efficient landings. Our exact scale relief models provided these, and saved lives by doing so.

I had contact with the inter-Allied and Service team set up specially for this work. It included Sarah Oliver, Churchill's daughter. She was an adept air photography interpreter and livened up the team no end with her wit and elegance. One day when she'd been working on models for the planned North African landings, Sarah had a 48-hour leave and went to Chequers, where her father so often spent a night or two away from Downing Street. She was comfortably settled in a big chair when her father came in. As usual, Churchill prowled around, puffing at his cigar. They were alone.

One a.m. struck, and Churchill announced with gravity that at this very moment under cover of darkness, 643 ships carrying Allied troops were approaching the shores of Africa. 'Six hundred and forty-four,' came a voice from the depth of the chair. 'What's that?' asked the Prime Minister. 'I've been working on Torch (code name of the operation) for months,' replied Sarah. Churchill frowned down at her. 'Why didn't you tell me?' he asked. 'I was told not to mention it to anyone,' said Sarah. Her father smiled, then had the last word. 'S'pose you thought I didn't know.'

Sophisticated aerial photography was playing an increasing part in the war effort. Before Torch (November 1942) an ace British pilot from Gibraltar took amazing aerial pictures at 'roof-top' level of the *Jean Bart* in Casablanca, the newest battleship of the French Navy. Though cleverly camouflaged, four slim grey pencils pointing seaward were picked out on the enlargements – indicating 15-inch guns.

Dive bombers were sent in to deal with them from the USS *Ranger*, an American aircraft carrier, as she rode the Atlantic waves off Casablanca. But the fleet commander, Admiral Hewitt, instead of waiting for our photographic Intelligence at Gibraltar to send the results of the raid, started to approach Casablanca in his flagship. There came the shriek of approaching shells and two great geysers of water leapt sixty feet into the air, drenching the Admiral and his officers on the bridge. Eleven two-gun salvos from the *Jean Bart* straddled the American flagship as she quickly retired. Dive bombers from the *Ranger* went back into action to finish off the *Jean Bart*'s guns. After that, Admiral Hewitt set great store by Photographic Intelligence.

Providing materials for camouflage – often of a highly ingenious and sophisticated nature – was an important part of my work at the Ministry of Supply. As a boy and young man, I had always been interested in 'legerdemain' – conjuring, deception, cunning devices. I had never missed the 'magic shows' put on by Jasper Maskelyne in London. He was a marvellous illusionist.

In World War Two this great magician was made a major, and he and his 'gang' adapted his conjuring and illusionist expertise to the battlefield on a very large scale. Their 'magic' was used to mislead German aerial photography seeking intelligence on reconnaissance flights. And I became one of their chief suppliers.

Maskelyne's H.Q. was at the Camouflage Experimental

Station of the Royal Engineers. There he and his team created dummy tanks and dummy guns, along with dummy men. They even perfected operational dummy submarines and a battleship, anything to mislead the German reconnaissance planes and German Intelligence H.Q. In one special case with the help of mirrors he 'conjured' up thirty six tanks in the desert where in fact there was only one.

The value of his work was never better demonstrated than in an incident which occurred after the Germans occupied the Channel Islands in 1940. They found an English safecracker in jail there. Thinking he had every reason to loathe the British, and that he would make a useful agent, they put a proposition to him which he promptly accepted. He was fully trained by them in sabotage work, then, in December 1942, landed in England from a U-boat under the code name Zigzag (ZZ).

His first job was to disrupt the vital production of aircraft at de Havilland's plant at Hatfield. But Zigzag had other ideas. Regardless of his peacetime activities he had decided that his real allegiance was to England. So he went immediately to the police, to whom he was well known for his felonies. They passed him on to the Double-Cross (XX) section of M.I.5., who were delighted to receive him. There was only one snag.

In order that he could be used for the rest of the war as a XX agent, he had first to convince his German 'employers' that he was a useful and successful operative. But this meant carrying out his first assignment, which was to blow up the power-house of the de Havilland plant, and to radio back after accomplishing it.

It was at this highly tricky moment that Maskelyne was called in and a scheme devised. In one of the three factories being used he built papier-maché dummies to look like pieces of broken generators. These were strewn with smashed bricks, blocks of concrete and other rubble around the powerhouse. A big relief canvas was made to cover the whole plant, painted to look from the air as if the place had been blown to Kingdom Come. ZZ then radioed to Germany: 'Mission accomplished.'

The following day, a German plane reconnoitred and photographed the damaged plant, or rather Maskelyne's masterpiece. The double-agent safe-breaker received a warm signal of praise from his German instructors. ZZ became a most useful man to XX.

Maskelyne was used in the D-day landing in Normandy in June 1944. This was the greatest deception and most important of all. Following Maskelyne's inspiration, and using my materials, false airfields were laid out filled with masses of dummy planes, dummy lorries, dummy landing craft and dummy military equipment in Kent, opposite the area of the Pas de Calais. The Germans were convinced we would attack at this short crossing. Their crack forces were concentrated there. When they heard reports of Allied Forces landing on the Normandy beaches they scoffed at these – believing them to be mere diversions, instead of the other way about. It gave us vital time to establish our position.

I was delighted to work on these projects for my old schoolboy hero, and managed to provide him with a great deal of new material from which he constructed his vast and marvellous camouflages. But getting hold of supplies on such a large scale was no easy task.

6

HIDE ME A COMPASS

I HADN'T BEEN installed in my 'Q office' at Portland House more than a few days before I received a telephone call which left me in no doubt as to the nature of my future work. 'M.I.9 here,' said a voice, 'I hear you're the new supply chap we're to deal with in future. Hope you've settled in. Now, I want to come and see you.' When he came, he asked me if it was possible to hide a small compass in a fountain pen. 'Our air chaps are screaming for them. Could you see if it can be done successfully, and if so get a few over to us as soon as possible?' He added a shade apologetically: 'I'm afraid it is rather urgent, we've promised Air Ministry we'll get something to them in a week or so. Do your best, will you?'

I wasn't at all sure that my best would be enough. With no experience of getting hold of ordinary supplies in wartime, let alone undercover, secret devices which could not easily be detected, I felt hopelessly out of my depth. Only one thing to be done, I told myself: get on with it. My visitor had been Major Clayton Hutton from Beaconsfield.

How was it to be done? Obviously, the makers of fountain pens were the most likely prospect, so I looked one up in the classified telephone directory and rang up their managing director. 'This is the Ministry of Supply,' I said, 'I'd like to come and see you about a rather tricky little design which would mean adapting one of your pens. When would be convenient?' Years of dealing with Arabs, who have to be told exactly what to do (and often how to do it) came to my aid in these early assignments, giving me an authority I was far from feeling. However, the director raised no objection on the telephone.

When I went round to see him I found a man who obviously was unused to moving towards any goal at anything but the most comfortably sluggish speed. He heard what I wanted – without, I fervently hoped, any clue as to its secret use (I merely told him we needed a hollow compartment left in the head, with a screwed-on lid made from the top of the cap). He nodded several times, looked slightly dazed, and said he'd certainly think about it. Experience would have told me that this process would never yield results in the time allowed, but experience was what I lacked. When I found that he was still cogitating with no result in sight the following day, I realised that I had made an initial error and lost twenty-four precious hours. Without telling him, I immediately contacted a rival firm of his and put the request to them, with a guarded hint that the Ministry which I represented 'would gladly deal with the first to come up with a suitable product'.

That did it. I was invited round immediately to discuss details with their top technical designer. In a matter of hours he was showing me a prototype which had been mocked-up in their design shop and which provided adequate space, I felt, for a tiny compass (if such a one could be found – I'd left pursuit of that till I knew exactly what its dimensions would have to be). Unfortunately, the joint of the screw cap was plainly visible, and I now faced the somewhat delicate task of revealing to the firm's enthusiastic managing director, a Mr. A.E. Andrews, why this ruled it out.

This was the first time I'd had to swear a supplier to

absolute secrecy. It gave me a strange feeling of cloak-and-dagger power to produce a copy of the Official Secrets document and request his signature to it. Had I but known, this man and his firm, Mentmore Manufacturing Company Ltd. of Platignum House, were to be among my most loyal and conscientious supporters throughout the war. On that first meeting I thought I was taking a big risk. So one of his fountain pens had to be put to official and highly secret use. Mr. Andrews signed with a flourish; I then told him the true purpose of my visit.

I also explained the vital need for inconspicuousness in the 'Q pen'. A pilot's life could depend on it. Once he understood this, Mr. Andrews promised to have a much less detectable model perfected by morning 'even if it takes me all night!' His zeal impressed me enormously (and opened the way to a friendship which lasted until his death in 1979). I had barely arrived in my office the following morning before he was on the phone announcing that he'd got the problem licked. What I saw in his hand a few minutes later was a pen in which the tell-tale crack was hidden completely by the rim of a mushroom-headed cap. Ordinary eyesight could never pick it out.

It was the most marvellous achievement, as were all the subsequent hundreds of such pens he produced to my order. I can't recall ever having to send even one back due to defective workmanship.

Like all fountain pens, these had a tubular rubber sac inside to hold the ink. As my confidence grew and the demand for more and more secret hiding places increased with the pace and complexity of the intelligence war, I examined this more carefully. 'Could you, do you think, shorten the rubber sufficiently to give me half an inch play at the far end?' I asked Andrews. He smiled wryly. 'Very easily,' he said. 'The only problem is that we pride ourselves on the ink-carrying capacity of our pens. You're going to ruin our reputation!'

I doubt if we did. My idea had been to secrete a paper-thin map printed on the finest tissue in the aperture thus won from the sac. Airmen finding their way back to us after bailing out in enemy territory, or forced landing in some remote corner of the continent, were, I'm pretty sure, far too grateful to be critical of the shortage of ink in their 'Q pens'. I was equally grateful to my resourceful supplier when he promptly adapted my idea and turned out hundreds of the little jobs.

The same firm made a rather natty little propelling pencil, one of which I bought for my own use. It was only when I got it home that I realised its potential value as a 'carrier'. Round the revolving shaft inside the barrel of the pencil was enough space to wrap a much larger, more extensive map than the one hidden in the pens. As an added refinement to both pen and pencil, which we supplied in sets where necessary, Andrews fitted a magnetized clip. The object of this, as explained to the flying crews before they took off on any operations over enemy territory, was to act as an emergency compass. Should the one packed in the cap go astray, or fail to operate, all they had to do was to balance the clip on a pin, or any fine point, and it would then automatically swing towards magnetic north.

My S.O.E. contact, who was a major customer of mine for the 'Q-pens' and pencils, confided to me (in a rare burst of chattiness) that my use of these simple gadgets had set their minds on a more lethal course. 'We tried fitting them with a small charge to fire gramophone needles,' he said one day. 'Could have made a useful nuisance-weapon, we thought. But we had to abandon the idea for fear of reprisals, unfortunately.' Today's terrorist organisations, I am told, have also adapted the harmless-looking pocket pen and pencil: packed full of plastic explosive, they are sufficient to blow the pressure doors off an airliner, ideal for an aerial hi-jack. By comparison with such diabolical deeds, my small contribution seems almost amateurish; but I believe quite a number of our R.A.F. aircrews were grateful for it.

Magnets were used in other ways, too. S.O.E. agents operating clandestine radio transmitters from isolated French, Italian and Yugoslavian farmhouses knew that German Gestapo and S.S. units were equipped to monitor electricity in their vicinities and to detect thereby the massive upsurge in power which radio transmission occasions. By holding a powerful magnet against the face of the farmer's electricity meter, it was possible to stop its circular motion entirely. No electricity, rather than too much, became the give-away while broadcasts were in progress; but the Germans never discovered the ruse. And some of the agents who survived still preserve, I believe, their life-saving magnets – though not, I am sure, for use on their domestic current!

To get back to 'the voice' from M.I.9 and his urgent need for compass-containing fountain-pens, I had not overlooked the fact that no compass as yet existed that was small enough to fit into the tiny aperture my friend Mr. Andrews had hollowed out for me. One had to be manufactured at top speed. I tracked down a couple of back-alley brothers working in a small factory at Clerkenwell. They had a contract to make large compasses for the Royal Navy and were amused when I said that I wanted them to turn over to making one smaller than they had ever seen or heard of. The maximum diameter, I told them, must not be more than one quarter of an inch.

The brothers – Barker was their name, (the whole firm consisted of no more than six men) – looked at each other with raised eyebrows. Fortunately, they saw my request as a challenge to their professional talents and undertook it immediately. The first sample they brought me was a brilliant little piece of engineering ingenuity and I was only too happy to give them an official order to proceed with the entire delivery. My mini-compasses were regularly and continuously re-ordered from this helpful source throughout the war.

Once it had been explained to me that a compass is only a magnetised piece of metal pivoting on a point and answering the natural attraction of the magnetic North pole, I realised that any number of devices could be converted to become such an instrument in an emergency. We turned our attention to the more difficult task of concealment. A dentist friend of mine first suggested a hollowed-out gold tooth when talking about poisons. These I had no interest in, since I saw my job as being concerned with helping our chaps to live rather than die. But as a place to tuck away one of my minute compasses, it proved ideal.

By implanting them in the mouths of R.A.F. aircrews whenever they went to the dentist to have a tooth seen to, we managed to filter quite a few into the prison camps. The Germans never bothered to give dental treatment to our chaps unless requested, so they remained undetected. We used them most, I believe, with the R.A.F.'s pathfinder force, whose special training in low-level reconnaissance and target identification became such a vital weapon of our bomber forces. Losses of these men were especially costly. It cheers me to recall that several of their crack crews were able to evade capture and make their way back to Britain, and active service, with the aid of our secret gadgets.

We didn't overlook buttons, either. Many of our flying officers latterly walked around wearing blue battle-dress which held a variety of 'Q' gadgets hidden in it. It amuses me to think how some of their girlfriends would have felt about embracing their heroes had they known that one button of their tunics contained a compass, another a small explosive charge! Their caps, incidentally, were also walking escape-kit receptacles, once I had found a saw suitable for secreting in their badges.

This was called a Gigli, and its normal use was in delicate brain surgery. Being flexible, it could be hidden away without difficulty. I'm told that the strength and fine cutting edge of its teeth did magnificent work in helping escapers to cut themselves free from any number of obstructions. I used to spend quite a bit of spare time wandering round the London shops and stores with a weather eye open for useful gadgets of this sort. The Gigli caught my attention on one of these 'recce' trips into the West End. I spotted it in the boarded-up window of Weiss and Son Ltd. of Oxford Street, and promptly arranged to place an order with the makers.

Apart from officers' cap badges, I found that this thin but strong little instrument could be concealed quite passably in an ordinary shoe or bootlace. These were issued to other ranks among the aircrew who did not possess the heavy, braided cap-badges of officers.

We were particularly anxious to provide our most senior officers with the best escape kits possible, so as to facilitate any escape attempt they might be able to make. To this end I asked Gieves Ltd., the Bond Street uniform makers who primarily supplied officers of the Royal Navy, if they could incorporate my saws and compasses in their tailored garments as a matter of course. They were only too happy to oblige.

No senior or high-ranking officer of our forces, from then on, went un-equipped in this direction. We even found an ingenious method of incorporating a Gigli saw into a small shaving mirror – thanks to a firm called Halex Ltd. It was tucked very carefully behind the rim. I've no doubt some of them are still there, probably being used by their owners with no knowledge of their secret content.

7

ESCAPE GAMES

I HAD A CALL from M.I.9 one morning, asking if there was anything I could do with hair-brushes. They were, of course, a natural item for any P.O.W. to have with him and had been used extensively in the first World War to conceal escape equipment. But the bristles were fixed in glue and the entire back of the brush was screwed or glued on. This meant that the screwed joint was readily visible, and if glued the entire back of the brush had to be destroyed to get to the secrets within. It was all too obvious, and I was sure the Germans were on to it.

I took the problem to G. B. Kent & Sons at Hemel Hempstead. Their experts came up with a wonderful brush for me in no time at all. It appeared to be all in one piece, but could be opened – rather like a Chinese puzzle – in such a way that nobody who did not know its secrets could possibly have come upon them by accident. The back was hollowed out to hold a compass, a large map and a nine-centimetre ridged, double-edged saw. The joint was hidden by a coating of dandruff. It was a most ingenious gadget but, unfortunately, had to be hand-made. Production was therefore restricted to only one or two a week.

So, after determining that Kent had just about run out of alternative ideas, I went to a London manufacturer, Marsh Ltd., whom I knew to be a small speciality firm with plenty of 'go'. I told them to develop a 'Q' hairbrush that was completely resistant to discovery. My man there suggested a novelty which he later developed most successfully. The brush had a beautifully disguised detachable panel in one side. Pulled out, this disclosed a deep cavity between the bristles and the back of the brush. It was excellent for holding almost anything.

As a matter of fact I still have one in my possession, and far from being obsolete it comes in handy whenever I travel abroad. I use it as a safe-deposit in which to tuck away bank notes and traveller's cheques. So cleverly constructed is it that I sometimes have to stop and think for a moment just how to open the darn thing!

My compasses hidden in buttons may have been rarely used, but they were a comforting accompaniment to many a bomber crew enduring heavy flak miles from home on a dark night, or beset by hostile fighters over enemy territory. One or two episodes involving them have made me grateful for the ingenuity of those suppliers of mine who worked so patiently and long on their development. In particular was the magnificent achievement of one of our flying aces, Group Captain Pickard.

Pickard was forced to ditch his bomber in the English Channel after he had been badly shot up during a raid. Unable to maintain height, he signalled the crew to prepare for a rough landing and put the plane into a shallow dive. Luckily the waves were not high enough to turn his aircraft over and he managed to keep it afloat long enough for the entire crew to bail out. They took to the one inflatable rubber dinghy unholed by bullets or shrapnel and unshipped the paddles. The question was, which way to head?

All round was a grey vista of choppy water; not a boat or a coastline in sight, no sun or stars. Without a compass bearing, it was as likely that they would end up on the occupied French coast as back in England. But Pickard's magic button saved the day. Fortunately, he had taken the trouble to learn his escape drill thoroughly.

He held the 'Q button' by its base, unscrewed the R.A.F. crested top, and revealed one of my little direction-finders sitting snugly inside. After fourteen hours of paddling, the entire crew landed on the Kentish coast – exactly on the course set by a needle less than half an inch in length, but working perfectly. This story gives me a great deal of satisfaction.

So I'm personally grateful to those little gadgets, for making it possible for me to feel that at least some of my deceptive devices were of real value in saving lives and helping our war effort. It is a feeling marred only by one incident. We found, to my disgust, that a well-known firm of jewellers had somehow got hold of one of my buttons and was copying them to sell at a vast profit. Just in time to prevent this, I organised a raid on their premises which nearly put them out of business, a fate they richly deserved in my opinion. Six of their copies had already been sold to R.A.F. personnel (who would have been issued with them anyway whenever necessary) and a further batch, I was told, was about to be made up in solid gold for lucrative export to the United States as 'war curios'. Nothing angered me more than such barefaced profiteering with one of our vital tools of the secret war.

It is only fair to point out that the Air Ministry did not altogether rely on 'Q factors', or depend on the work of my suppliers and me to save as many of their shot-down aircrews as possible. They published detailed instructions on how to improvise a compass from any common article made of steel or ferrous metal. To magnetise such items as razor blades (balanced on a pin, these became ideal compass needles), it was necessary, however, to pass an electric current through them, while wound with fifteen turns of lighting flex or similar. A 12-volt car battery was all one needed for this. But to a man on the run it was seldom easy to find such an accessory, so my ready-made miniatures were welcomed.

Having pointed the way home, the next task was to provide route maps. Again, in most cases these had to be ultra-small for packing in tiny, secret hideaways. But experience and commonsense convinced me that there was no need to make *all* 'Q gadgets' equally clandestine: the more obvious some of them were the more likely they were to fool the Germans. I therefore printed a number of my larger maps on ordinary handkerchieves, the kind anyone – even German prison guards – might use to blow their noses. I did so in invisible ink, of course, but only when I had discovered a variety of this which would not suddenly and dangerously reveal itself on being held up to the light, or moistened. One ink I used quite extensively required urine to make it reappear – a choice I thought highly sensible, since that liquid was seldom likely to be in short supply.

For maps hidden inside gadgets we had to think of something else. A pure silk fabric and a non-rustling rag tissue of the finest paper imaginable were obviously suitable materials. The latter, specially made for the job, was magnificent. Nylon came along in the latter stages of the war, with the entry of the Americans. The real poser was how to secrete these flimsy, beautifully printed little miniature works of art inside such limited spaces as we had at our command. I was not a pipe smoker, but I knew many of our prisoners were (from the amount of pipe tobacco requested to be included in the parcels delivered to them by the Red Cross). This set me thinking.

A pipe is a nice, large and somewhat mysterious object. It is capable of containing a number of secret drillings and chambers. The trouble with it is that it tends to become an incinerator when carrying out its normal function of burning tobacco. Could an asbestos lining, I asked my pipe-manufacturing suppliers, be made to encase the bowl, allowing space between this and the wooden walls to take my maps?

It was all a matter of thickness, they said. And, of course, though they did not say so, it meant ruining the pleasurable qualities of their famous pipes. I asked them to produce one for me and have it tried out. After a heavy pipe smoker on their staff had smoked the thing into near-red heat, I was shown the map. Withdrawn from the asbestos protective coating, it was almost as good as new.

Smaller maps and compasses could also be concealed inside the stem of the pipe. Where the larger maps hidden in the bowl could only be extracted by destroying the pipe, these were easily accessible. I decided the 'Q pipes' should be sent in whenever possible.

But only the best briarwood, grown in Germany (and now virtually unobtainable in Britain), would stand up to the complex drillings and heat involved. Ordinary cherry wood, such as was being used as a substitute by British manufacturers in wartime, would not do at all. The problem held me up completely until I ran into a fellow who owned a large London shoe-firm.

I knew he was trading with enemy suppliers, with official permission to do so. There was a special government office sanctioning such operations, designated the 'Trading With the Enemy Department'. I suggested that he might be able to obtain the briarwood I wanted and he readily agreed, but explained that it would take time. I told him to go ahead.

Meanwhile, I heard from the directors of one of the large tobacco firms I had already approached that supplies of briar had been located via their contacts in the Argentine. It meant that my enemy-trading friend was left sitting with a very valuable load of this unobtainable wood to the vast discomfort of his competitors. They could only see that the government had allowed him to obtain highly profitable materials which were forbidden to them, and howls of anguish and anger reached me.

It put me in a bit of a spot. I couldn't take the wood

myself. Nor could I very well stop him selling it at a profit. I eventually compromised by suggesting to him that, in return for his windfall, he should donate £10,000 to the Red Cross who were doing so much good work for the P.O.W.s. He ruefully agreed to this, and at least my conscience was clear.

The Red Cross parcels were a tempting vehicle for deliveries of our secret gadgets to the prison camps, but we made it a rule never to tamper with food parcels. Had we once abused the international undertaking in regard to these, and been found out, none of these welcome gift packages would have been allowed to reach our men at all. Our aim was to increase morale, not to destroy it. So the Red Cross was never put at risk by my activities, much as I hankered after its easy access to my target areas.

There were, however, other parcels and pieces of equipment which could be sent into the camps. Games were usually tolerated. I had a very cunning accomplice in this department, a young Frenchman named Monsieur A. Journet, of Journet and Sons Ltd. Journet had the mind of a master escapologist: he thought up the most brilliant hiding places and an extraordinary number of devious springs and catches to enable the secret chambers to be revealed.

Through him, I managed to create an array of trick chessmen, draft pieces and playing cards which a Houdini might have admired. Special inks for forging false documents were also in demand by the camp escape committees, I was told by my M.I.9 contact one day. We promptly got in touch with Journet who had a chessman on my desk in less than a week containing a watertight compartment to hold the necessary liquid. The piece was a knight, and to open the 'bottle' it was necessary to unscrew the horse's head. But in a clockwise direction – a trick of mine he had adapted successfully.

Dominoes were another useful carrier. Hollowed out,

the box-like pieces became excellent if rather too obvious containers. Waddingtons, the games people, also found a way of inserting silk-tissue maps in the backs of playing cards which was especially favoured by my contacts at M.I.9 and M.I.6, though for some reason which I never fully understood. Perhaps Ridley and his opposite number were keen bridge players. That wouldn't surprise me, as quite a few of the stunts these master deceivers got up to were similar in inspiration to the higher forms of that complex game. I myself took a keen interest in diverting secret supplies and equipment into theatrical 'props' and effects, which I found I could do with the help of some of the better stage-craft manufacturing firms. They entered into the subterfuge game with great enthusiasm, as one might have expected.

We thereupon produced a number of highly ingenious fake beards, make-up sticks and the like with carefully hidden compasses, maps, saws and other escape material in them. Provided we could rely on our own M.I.9 agents to inform the escape committees there was no problem about our gadgets being overlooked.

8

CUTTING RED-TAPE

I CONFESS TO having been bothered – not a little, sometimes – by the civil service mentality, which seemed to me to be working at snail's pace during most of the war. I understand that they had all been going along at their own speed when the war had shattered their well-ordered lives. No doubt it had been hard to adjust to, and some plainly had decided that they couldn't, or wouldn't, cope. But from time to time I would find real fury mounting in me over the frustrating red tape which wound itself round my ankles whenever I tried to stride at more than regulation pace.

Rummaging around second-hand shops in search of European suitcases, I once came across an ideal representation of this state of mind: a picture of sleek cows sitting in a field, listlessly chewing the cud. Having bought it and hung it on my office wall opposite my desk, I added underneath in Arabic (which nobody in the building could translate) 'Civil Service'.

To have to acknowledge the importance of having everything done in quadruplicate at least was one thing. But when men and women were risking their brave necks for us civilian officials, I found it hard to stomach some of the unnecessary delays. A safety-valve had to be found, and I located it in my favourite indoor sport, squash. For twenty minutes or so two or three times a week I'd work the anger out of my system by imagining the squash-ball to be the round head of the Minister of Economic Warfare; or of some other chap whose department had put a brake on my activities. After pounding away at these surrogate adversaries in this relatively harmless way I found I was able to put up with most things.

A particular bugbear was the way my costs were persistently queried for what seemed to me wholly obstructive and pettyfogging reasons. I sensed that behind these probes was a jealous feeling among my inquisitors that I, a mere wartime 'temp', was being granted far too much liberty and independence. The need was felt to clip my wings and on several occasions this seriously hampered my war effort. I was forced to spend futile time and energy in ridiculous arguments. Quite often these involved delay in settling with loyal suppliers of my goods – people I had persuaded to turn their hands to my requirements as a matter of the utmost urgency.

There seemed no valid excuse for such niggardly behaviour. Of course, the Treasury officials concerned knew nothing of my secret function; but they at least knew that I had the authority of the Ministry behind me, and that I could hardly be placing such orders as I was without due regard for financial considerations.

I once had to put through an invoice for several packets of razor blades. Each packet was supposed to contain twelve blades, though in fact each included a miniature but serviceable razor and soap as well as three blades (magnetised to act as compasses when balanced on a matchstick) with which a bearded or moustachioed agent or escaper could alter his appearance radically in a matter of moments.

Naturally, these had had to be specially made by one of the major firms capable of producing such delicate instruments. Thus the bill, which I initialled and passed for payment, was for 'special' – and I underlined it, knowing the density of skull in the Treasury department which would have to settle the account. I had asked the managing director of the firm making them to turn aside from vital defence commitments to make them for me.

The Treasury nearly had a fit when they saw the cost of each packet. If nothing else, they knew what razor blades should cost. How could I possibly justify, I was asked over the phone, such an outrageous piece of obvious profiteering at the Ministry's expense? In vain did I try to get it across to my angry superior that these were no ordinary blades. 'These are *special* jobs, don't you see?' I finally shouted. 'They're not run-of-the-mill blades at all!' He was silent for a moment, then with monumental and crushing dignity, he replied: 'I say, Fraser-Smith, I hope you know what you're doing. We can't afford *luxuries* these days, you know.'

I bottled my rising wrath and let him lecture me for a good five minutes. If taking a rocket now and then was part of my job, then it had to be borne. But before I put down the telephone I decided to try, at least, to put my point across. If the Treasury was not satisfied, as plainly they were not, why not send a costing clerk round with the invoice, I suggested? Let me take him down to the firm which had supplied the blades for an on-the-spot investigation of their charges. That way, surely, we would soon discover whether or not there had been 'profiteering'? And if there had been, then we could take the firm to task, as well as myself, I implied.

He rose to the bait. A man was sent over, bearing the suspected bill. I took him to the firm's offices – having first ensured that he was already under the Official Secrets oath and satisfied myself that he was never likely to spill the beans. My instructions were straightforward: he was to go through the costing, item by item, with the finest toothcomb he could muster. I would be guided entirely by his results.

Needless to say, they were far from being as the Treasury had suspected. Detailed examination of the charges made to us, involving a time-study of the hours of labour and other factors involved, showed that we had been undercharged rather than the reverse. My supplier, out of the goodness of his patriotic heart, had deliberately taken not a penny of the regulation percentage of profit allowed to all outside firms supplying government or defence equipment.

Having seen this proved beyond doubt, I took the invoice from the hand of my Treasury companion and tore it up. 'Now please write out another bill for me,' I said to the surprised supplier. 'Only, this time, include your proper profit.' Seeing that I was in earnest – though baffled by my request – he did so. The embarrassed Treasury clerk then had to return to his department and confront my interrogator with an even larger bill, every item of which was fully justified. He never bothered me again.

It was later suggested that inasmuch as I was placing orders for millions of pounds of material, a high ranking civil servant should be placed in immediate charge over me. This was raised only once. The incident of the razor blades may have convinced my superiors that in order to function in a manner which would help, rather than hamper, the war effort it was necessary for me to maintain my flexibility. They took the point, and I was permitted – though grudgingly – to remain independent. This had both advantages and disadvantages.

One of the latter was that it was pointed out to me more than once that I might conceivably become the target of an assassination attempt, or even a kidnapping. I paid no attention until some of my more romantic, cloak-and-dagger-minded colleagues became insistent that the risk was not altogether bizarre.

I decided to arm myself with my small automatic pistol, and, as I was having a suit made at the time, asked the tailor to put in an extra little pocket suitable for carrying the weapon. I would also carry it under my arm, held in place with a belt; or sometimes rather loosely in my back pocket. It was only on rare occasions that I bothered to have the thing on my person at all, but there were times when it seemed advisable.

I didn't worry too much about German spies, since our people had done a marvellous job of rounding them all up early in the war. But once in a while I would notice a chap changing buses with me as I travelled around London. This made me cautious. I took the rudimentary precaution of at least being aware of a possibility of danger on this account, even though nothing ever really occurred. There was, in fact, more likelihood of my drawing the gun on some recalcitrant civil servant than on a German spy!

In order to function efficiently and more secretly, I had decided early on to become a telephone rather than a paper person. We eliminated files, kept our correspondence down to a mere fraction of what it might have become (mainly the sending out of orders and payment authorisations), and I must have made up to a hundred telephone calls a day tracking down the proper sources of my materials before going to see anybody about them. It saved a tremendous amount of time and made it possible for me to plan my 'rounds' so that I rarely wasted a visit.

In my pocket 'filing system' notebook I kept a detailed record in alphabetical order of all the firms with which I was actually doing business. A very simplified order form was used, giving nothing away. I never used 'secret' or 'special' on any document where it could be avoided, just a straightforward '100 hairbrushes' or whatever. In my notebook I used my own code system to distinguish between several similar-sounding devices. (For example, I had four different shaving-brushes based on different ideas in simultaneous production.)

The order could be filled in by me at the premises concerned during a personal visit, or sent on to the director. On receiving the goods, I merely initialled the top right-hand corner of the invoice and had it sent to the paying department of the M.O.S. to be forwarded to the Treasury. Thus nobody involved with the payment was aware that there was anything the least bit secret about it. Everything was, or seemed, innocent.

There was a time, short-lived as it turned out, when I found myself in some difficulty over the concealment of a certain piece of equipment. Lacking any means of making its receptacle appear to be no more than a normal item of everyday use, I turned in my dilemma to Customs and Excise. Those officers, I felt sure, had had plenty of experience of secret and clever hiding places for contraband. To my intense disappointment, however, nothing came of this. Either they were too canny to give away their dossier of dirty deeds to a civilian – even in wartime, and backed by Ministry authority – or they knew of nothing suitable for the minute items I was anxious to tuck away from sight and suspicion.

Security in my view is so much more a matter of common sense than any wizardry of sleuthing and undercover magic. The most obvious can often be the least detectable. Towards the end of the war I was told by one of my M.I.6 contacts of a purge of their offices in 54 Broadway by a security chap with a most officious air about him. All maps had to be removed from walls. Anything the least bit incriminating was to be taken away and hidden in locked drawers and filing cabinets. No reason was given, but that weekend the landlord of the premises – keen to re-let the building now that hostilities were coming to an end – showed round a delegation from the Russian Department of Trade! They had expressed interest (as well they might!) in acquiring the place.

When I heard about Kim Philby's espionage activities and later defection, it seemed unbelievable to me that all this was allowed to go on under the noses of our most secret Intelligence service. Philby was, as everybody now knows, in M.I.6 and worked at 54 Broadway. It is entirely probable that he, with consummate cheek (and not a little human psychology), had tipped off the Russian trade people to the coming availability of the building. (If, in fact, their 'bugging' of it had not already started. We were not alive to such electronic warfare devices in those days.)

Ours was a far more schoolboy type of security, which allowed for ludicrous overkill on occasion. A woman friend of mine, an artist, was seen to be sketching in the country near her home by zealously alert neighbours. They reported her to the police. An inspector found her sitting on a wall, making drawings of a nearby haystack. He had, of course, to make a full report. The closest my friend had come to any sensitive or military target was, he was able to record, the village pub which featured in the background of one of her works.

On another occasion, a clergyman I knew was told by a telephone operator, whom he had asked to put through an urgent call on Church business, that 'only official priority calls are being connected.' 'Ah yes,' said the cleric with some wit, 'but this is on behalf of the Almighty.' The well-trained girl consulted her list, then firmly informed him that she had no such name listed.

My PA-secretaries were always impressed with the strictest of security needs, as indeed was everyone working for government departments in wartime. I told my girls no more than was absolutely necessary of my clandestine role. It was therefore vital to my undercover security that they should toe the line. But one night I had a nasty shock.

I found, on asking for the key to my office which my secretary should have left at the door on leaving the building, that it was not with the security people responsible. It was only by chance – since I was fire-watching, and it was a quiet night with no raids in sight – that I'd sought it out. Its absence was alarming.

Could she still be at work? I rushed up to the first floor.

No, the door was locked and the place empty. I had only one way of getting inside, and this was by rousing the duty officer at the Military Intelligence headquarters who would have a duplicate key. But in doing so I would initiate a formidable inquiry into the reasons why our key was not in its proper place, since no keys at all were allowed out of our tightly-guarded buildings.

I knew well what that would mean. My girl would certainly be dismissed in short-order. She'd be out of a job, and I'd be without a first-class assistant who had proved herself the best I'd ever had. Two earlier girls had caused me quite a few problems, the first girl being a bit of a chatter-box, the second having lacked all the qualities I depended on to 'backstop' my strange activities.

Above all, I didn't want to have to train a new girl in my somewhat unorthodox ways of waging secret war. So, after a few moments thought, I hit on a plan. She'd have to be taught a lesson she'd never forget, assuming she was innocent of any deliberate breach, which I was sure she was. I rang her up. The security officer in charge of our building wanted to see her urgently, I said. By my watch, it was now after 11 o'clock, and she sounded anything but pleased. 'What for?' she asked. I kept my voice deliberately chilly and uncommunicative. 'That, I'm afraid, you'll have to worry about,' I told her mercilessly. 'But I am instructed to inform you that if you are not here before midnight you will be reported to the Chief. You know what that means, so I advise you most strongly to get down here right away. Take a taxi if necessary.' I hung up.

That summons scared the life out of her. She never made another slip. From then on she concentrated on every job I gave her with total responsibility until completed. After the war, she and her husband came to see me while on a cycling holiday, and I enjoyed a good chuckle with her over the incident. 'How is she with keys?' I asked her husband. But I didn't give away her guilty secret.

It is quite untrue that women cannot keep secrets. Some do so far better than men. Sir Henry Tizzard, Scientific Advisor to the Air Staff and Ministry of Defence, knew this. When his chief scientist confessed one day to being uneasy in discussing secrets in front of his secretary, Tizzard took him aside and gave him some very sound words of advice, in my opinion. He told him that in his experience women were more secure than men because men liked to brag that they were 'in the know', whereas women did not.

He explained that his own secretary had once told him that her father had not the ghost of an idea of what her work was. Tizzard decided to test her out. He asked the father what his daughter was doing and the man replied: 'Oh, the same old thing, you know. C.S.'

Well, 'C.S.' was how we referred to the highly secret department Tizzard's secretary did a lot of work for: the Government Code and Cypher School. So this was distinctly bad news. Tizzard waited with some impatience to tell his girl what her father had replied. She listened to him quietly, then burst out laughing. 'How marvellous,' she said. 'Poor old daddy was talking about our church: C.S.! We're all devoted Christian Scientists!'

Sir Henry, a remarkable man, delighted in telling the story against himself. He was a strict believer in security at all levels, and he firmly believed in the power of women to protect secrets – a view seldom echoed by my Civil Service colleagues in wartime. One wonders how the legendary secrets of the S.O.E. and of the code-breakers at Bletchley and Beaconsfield would have fared if any of those splendidly devoted women of the F.A.N.Y who were entrusted with them had breathed a word. A wartime slogan comes to mind: 'Be like dad, keep mum.' Amusing, but biased I'd say. Mum knew how to keep secrets too.

She knew a great deal more than that. What can one say of the women agents of S.O.E. who faced torture and death behind enemy lines? I have no adequate words of praise for their bravery, though I felt closer to them than most. We were all amateurs in the secret war against Hitler. How terrible to know that in our French Section of S.O.E. alone, twelve of the fifteen women captured (out of thirty-nine landed in occupied France) perished in concentration camps. The three survivors brought back horrifying tales.

These were attractive, feminine women mostly, in their twenties and thirties. My heart went out to them. The cover we could provide for their underground work seemed pathetically feeble. I did my best to find suitable clothing – involving myself in the purchase of secondhand French underwear, in which I had no knowledge of sizes or styles. I gathered also an assortment of French cosmetics.

These women went into battle as heroically as any man. They, and the F.A.N.Y. girls and women who worked with them as cypher and signals operatives, decoding and transmitting messages of the utmost urgency and secrecy, were a precious part of our secret forces. When war ended, Brigadier F.W. Nicholls sent each of them a message which, alongside a photograph of my containers dropping on parachutes through the skies over enemy territory, properly commended their bravery and dedication.

'You,' he wrote, 'were a member of a team which, by its faithful service to your comrades behind the enemy lines on the battle fronts of the world, enabled nations to retain their self respect, and made the Allied task so much easier. You have reason to be proud of your contribution to Victory.'

On the cover of the card containing this commendation were the following lines: 'Over the air came many noises, From the noises came many men, From the men came Liberty.' From the women, too, I would say. My hat is off to them.

9

DALTON'S FANATICS

ON THE 2nd of July, 1940, Hugh Dalton, the then Minister of Economic Warfare, wrote to Lord Halifax: 'We have to organize movements in enemy-occupied territory comparable to the Sinn Fein movement in Ireland. These must use many different methods, including industrial and military sabotage, terrorist acts and propaganda.

'What is needed is a new organization to co-ordinate, inspire, control, and assist the nationals of the oppressed countries. They must themselves be direct participants. We need absolute secrecy, a certain fanatical enthusiasm, willingness to work with people of different nationalities and complete political reliability. The organization should, in my view, be entirely independent of the War Office machinery.'

Two weeks later Churchill invited Dalton to start just such an operation. Its founding charter was signed by Neville Chamberlain (one of the few bright things he did in government in my view). It opened the way to the formation of one of the most glamorous, brave and self-sacrificing 'secret armies' of the war: Britain's Special Operations Executive, S.O.E. From the knowledge I had of their hazardous work, I should say that they were among the most illustrious of any who served this country in the dark years of the war. Imagine what it meant to be placed alone, virtually defenceless, inside enemy-occupied territory. The 'Baker Street Irregulars' (as S.O.E. were nick-named, due to their headquarters' address in London) recruited and trained men and women who faced this as an accepted duty. It was a task calling for extraordinary courage. The risk of immediate death on capture was bad enough. But S.O.E.'s agents knew that they also faced the likelihood of torture devised by the devil himself.

Hugh Dalton had not been strong enough to convince the doubting Thomases who opposed the establishment of this *franc tireur* force. Its control therefore was soon handed over to a military man, one who could do battle with the conventional wisdom of the War Cabinet. (Dalton had not even occupied a seat on it.) Ideal for this challenging assignment was Major-General Sir Colin Gubbins, a fiery and hard-headed Scot. He quickly formed S.O.E. into a major extension of the European fighting forces and proved that 'irregular' as they were, under his command they could also perform tasks of the utmost value.

I felt a total dedication to those agents of S.O.E., 480 in all, whose average life in the field narrowed down to a mere three weeks, as we later discovered. Some were picked up as they landed; many were betrayed by German sympathisers; others were never heard from after they bailed out; but they were all magnificent. The weight of responsibility resting on the shoulders of men like Gubbins and Buckmaster (head of the large French section) and other heads of S.O.E. sections for the occupied European countries must have been appalling. As for me, I was extremely careful about every item I was asked to provide for them.

Supplying S.O.E., in fact, was a mammoth task. Every item had to be precisely accurate since the smallest error could cost a life. I spent a lot of time in the Paddington area of London, wandering around second-hand shops. I was looking for French clothing of all sorts, and various sizes of continental suitcases. In those days our radio equipment was so bulky, and came in so many sizes, that luggage had to be provided which would accommodate not only clothes but all our operative gadgets as well. The Germans were capable of the most minute checks on anyone they suspected of being an agent.

By arrangement I was given advance notice of all auction sales of railway lost property. This enabled me to take my pick of foreign luggage. Anything I selected was paid for by the Treasury at an agreed price. In time, it became a practice for the railway people to contact me whenever a foreign valise turned up among the items abandoned or lost in their trains. If I accepted it and subsequently its owner came to reclaim it, I made arrangements for a new case to be supplied in its place, with a suitable excuse (damage due to bombing, etc.). I've no doubt the owner was quite happy with the exchange.

I also collected a number of well-worn valises from Frenchmen who had fled from the German occupation. They too received brand new British leather cases in exchange, without ever realising to what they owed their good fortune.

Accessories were a problem. By a stroke of good luck, I found a chap in London who had made a collection of every European hair and shaving brush in existence – an amazing sight. He loaned them to me to have copied, as did the match firm of Bryant and May with their splendid collection of foreign match-box labels.

Cloth, or the cut of a suit not made in whatever country the agents were operating, was quite sufficient to arouse the Germans' suspicions. I made it a rule never to provide clothing which was not sufficiently 'local' to pass muster under the most searching scrutiny, and wherever possible the real thing. Watches, garments, shoes, even the labels on suitcases had to be just right. The Free French H.Q. in London were extremely helpful here: they introduced me to English importers who still held stocks of genuine French-made boots and shoes. When I needed authentic ration cards and other documents for their country, S.O.E. handled the forgeries from paper which I supplied, since the Germans were constantly changing identity papers.

When I lacked up-to-date information, they obtained it from the continent for me. In a day or so, I could always count on the right data turning up. The support of these loyal Frenchmen who had fled with de Gaulle from the Nazi invaders of their country was wholehearted and invaluable.

But apart from I.D. cards and ration books, I still had to find a number of other 'Q factors' which S.O.E. agents could carry with confidence, knowing that they were extremely unlikely to arouse suspicion. One of their most dangerous items of equipment was the note-paper they had to have in order to retain a mass of often technical information discovered in the course of their activities. Paper for this had not only to be sturdy enough to withstand rough treatment and adverse weather conditions, but also instantly destructible. I had two ways of accomplishing this feat.

I could supply a completely edible paper, tough but palatable, so that a suspect or accosted agent could make a meal of his notes, swallowing them after a few quick bites. Rice paper made this possible, and a well-known firm came up with the goods for me when I went to them with the problem. How many times secret messages were chewed and swallowed during the war in this way (without the slightest gastronomic ill-effect, so far as I know!) is hard to say. But beyond doubt many agents could be grateful to my suppliers for their efforts.

My other method of getting rid of paper quickly was more flamboyant but still effective. We developed a flash paper which when ignited simply disappeared without trace. No smoke or ash. I believe the secret was to implant magnesium in the paper's fabric, but exactly how it was done and what other ingredients were used I have no idea. What I do know is that we supplied literally tons of both rice and flash papers during the war. Most of them went to S.O.E., but M.I.6 took quite a bit as well. There must have been a steady demand for secret 'read-and-destroy'-type messages in more than one field of Intelligence operations.

Another vital need of the S.O.E. man or woman, dropped or landed in enemy territory and posing as a native, was the right form of money. Old, obsolete notes or coins could unmask an agent faster than displaying the Union Jack. Fortunately, we had a large supply of both French and German currency tucked away in banks and elsewhere during the early stages of the campaign. But this, of course, had to be replaced as soon as it was changed. And the Germans were very quick to do that without the least warning.

The answer lay in counterfeiting our own supplies: we became expert 'coiners' for this reason. Even the great and highly respected firm of Waterlow, printers of British bank-notes, proved more than capable of turning their hands to this nefarious enterprise. Such German money as we could not obtain from my shady Argentine contacts and others was beautifully forged, I can now reveal, largely on their presses. I used their skills in other, less dubious, ways as well, notably the making of maps; but the notion of these reputable experts entering the murky world of forgery, though entirely for patriotic reasons, still tickles my sense of the bizarre.

I might add that S.O.E. had their own counterfeiting set-up in the basement of the Science Museum in Kensington. They, too, became adept at forging passes, I.D.s, ration books, and all the other documents needed. Some of these had to be completed on the spot, since they required exact dates. But, in general, it was comparatively easy for us to supply the S.O.E. for their operations in France, because we had such good liaison with the Free French resistance forces. It was mainly in Germany that we found it impossible, and the forgery there was left to people on the ground.

Many of the P.O.W. camps also developed very skillful forgers who took care of their own needs. I don't believe we ever actually infiltrated forgers into the camps for the express purpose of plying their trade for the benefit of the escape committees, but, as was so often the case, talented people of all sorts rose to the occasion. Certainly a good number of young P.O.W.s discovered a talent for counterfeiting and forgery that they never knew they possessed. Whether any of them pursued this particular line of work after the war, I wouldn't know; but I'd be surprised if none took it up as a result.

The Germans knew what we were up to, of course. They kept changing every piece of documentation as often as they possibly could. Not only I.D.s and ration cards, but even railway tickets were subject to overnight alteration and substitution. They knew that the most damning giveaway of any spy or escaper was to be caught with false papers or out-dated documents. Even food ration coupons had to be attended to very carefully for this reason.

Looking back, it seems to me now that S.O.E.'s way of working behind enemy lines was as unorthodox as Sherlock Holmes's attitude towards crime. Colin Gubbins ran the show on totally unconventional lines. I was amazed by the different kinds of people he had working for him, not only as agents but instructors. For instance, the best people he could find to advise on sabotage were insurance adjusters. These, he discovered, had had more opportunity than most of gaining an insight into the practical side of the subject, though from the other side of the fence. They knew exactly what it took to put a machine out of action.

Even more to the point, Gubbins recruited criminals to teach his agents the best way to crack safes, rob banks, and carry out burglary. Notorious counterfeiters trained his agents in the forgery they needed to survive. And I am quite sure that it was not patriotism alone which Gubbins appealed to in these men. The added perk of a reduced sentence (even, in some instances, complete remission) may well have provided additional persuasion.

So, kitting out and equipping S.O.E. was a joint effort. Supplying their agents with up-to-the minute materials, outwitting an eternally suspicious enemy – whose slogan 'The enemy is listening' became our watchword too as regards internal security – was a continuous, vital process. Where Gubbins and his staff could provide, they did so. Where not, they came directly to me. Though originally a branch of M.I.6, hived off as a result of Dalton's accurate assessment of their independent functions, they tended to operate exclusively and apart from the other Intelligence sections. I learnt to anticipate their telephone orders by stockpiling as much civilian gear as possible from the various theatres. Indeed, as my secretary reminded me, at times my office looked like a jumble sale, with a strong smell of foreign tobacco, garlic and scent!

The entire S.O.E. operation under Gubbins was designed to create 'cells' of independent agents lacking any central organisation in the areas where they operated. Essentially it was the same technique as that employed today with such deadly effect by terrorist organisations. No treachery or indiscretion – by France's Vichy-ites for one, and many other Nazi sympathisers elsewhere – could result in the whole network of agents being rounded up, for the simple reason that the right hand rarely knew what the left hand was doing. No single agent knew the whereabouts of more than one or two 'contacts'. His main connection, as the war developed, was with underground and resistance forces in occupied countries.

France's Resistance Force was fundamentally different from the *maquis,* who were underground fighters pure and

1 Shaving brushes were invaluable containers. A tightly rolled map and compass, or Minox film, were hidden in the stem. The secret compartment was revealed by turning the stem on a reverse thread. If one tried to unscrew it one just closed it more tightly.

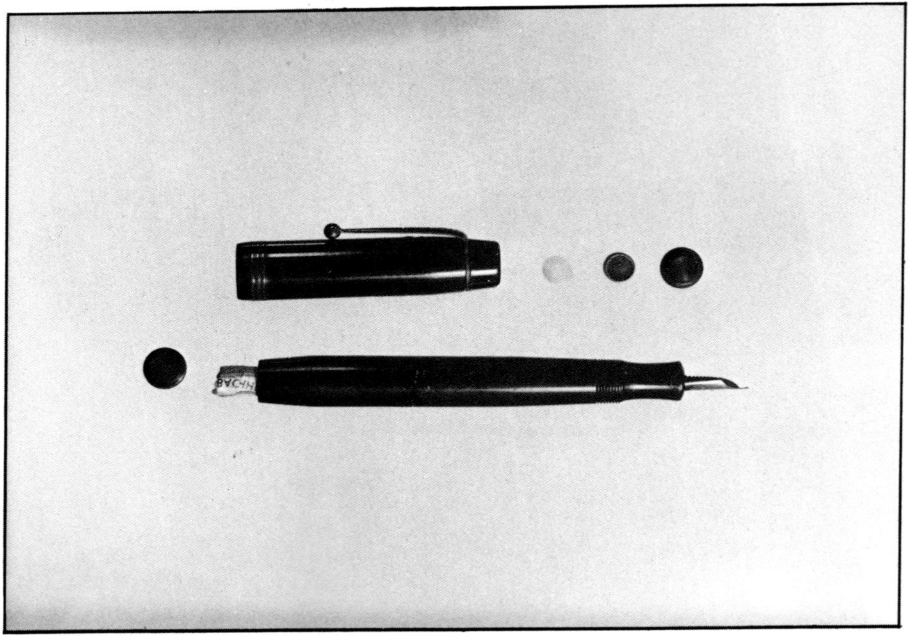

2 The fountain pen held a compass in a hollow compartment (left) in the head. The mushroom-headed cap concealed the vital joint. Later the ink-sac was reduced in size and a paper-thin map was secreted in the space gained.

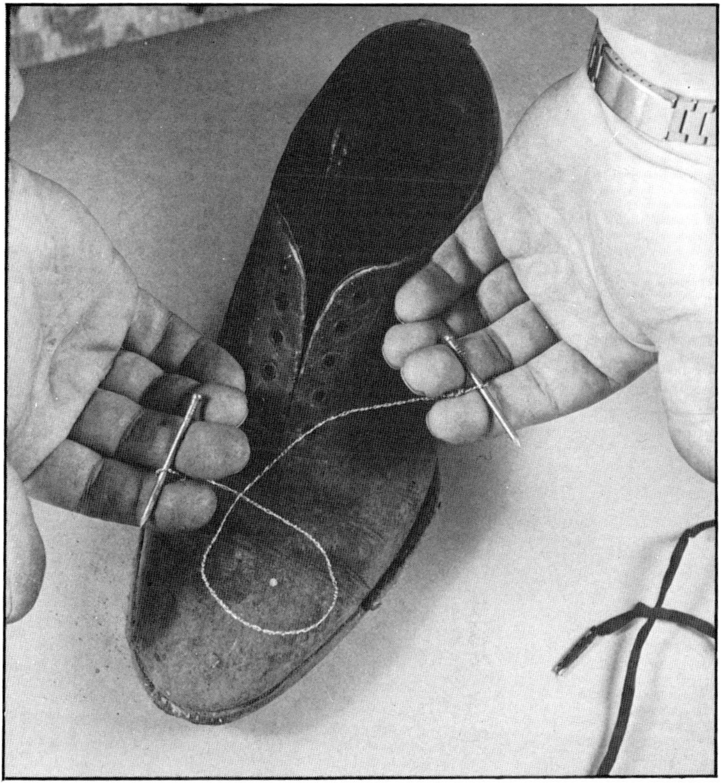

3 A Gigli—a flexible surgical saw—could be concealed in an ordinary boot or shoe lace. It could also be hidden in cap badges.

4 (A) The 1914–18 war hair brush showed the screw joints for removing the back and revealing the secrets inside.
(B) This brush of World War II appeared to be all in one piece but those who knew its secret could remove the centre block of bristles revealing (C) a 9 cm double edged saw, a compass and a silk rag-tissue map.
(D) This brush looked normal but had a well-designed panel which when pulled out (E) disclosed a deep cavity between the bristle and the brush's back.

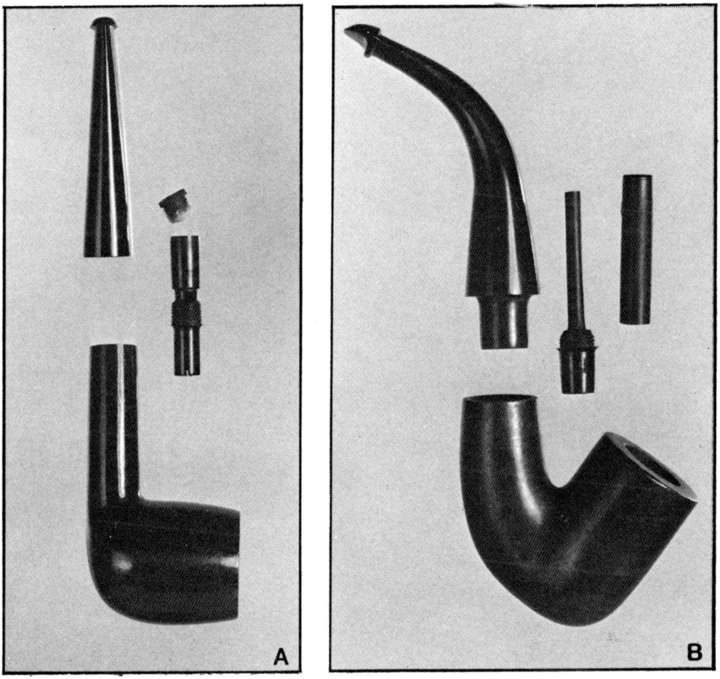

5 All sorts of objects were used to carry the silk rag-tissue maps. Pipes (A & B) were capable of containing secret messages, a minute compass, and a map concealed within the asbestos lined bowl.
(C) Dominoes sent to prisoners-of-war and SOE Agents were useful carriers.

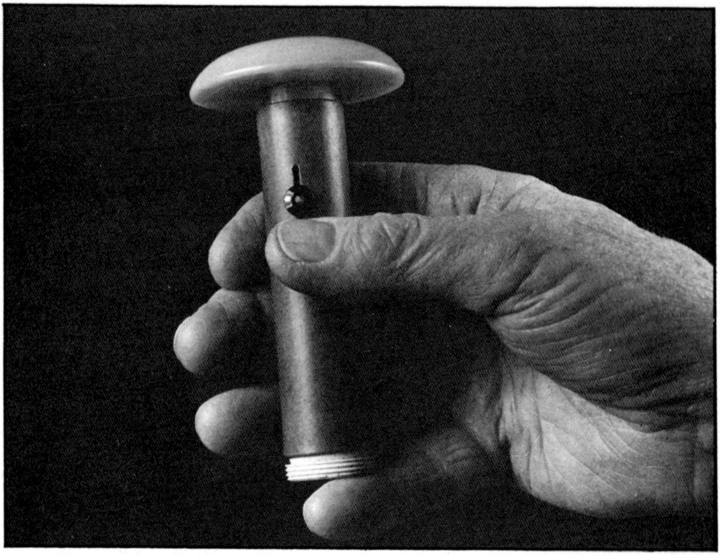

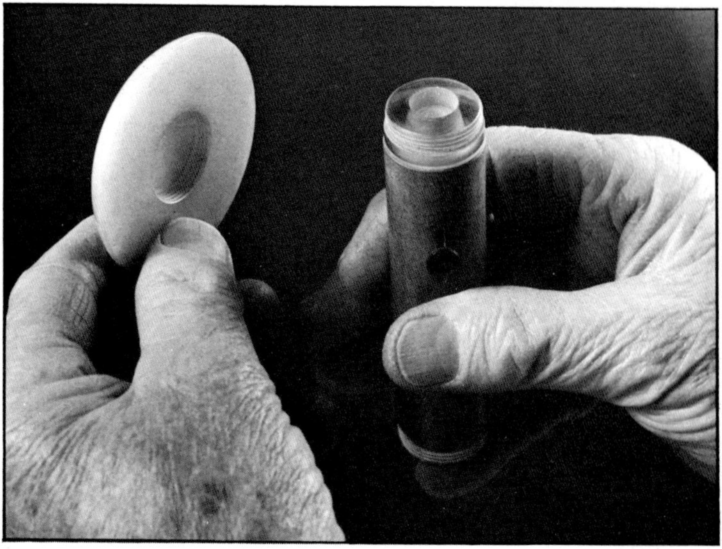

6 R.A.F. pilots need landing lights which could be seen clearly from above but not from the surrounding country-side. Light from these torches was diffused by a mushroom-shaped dome of thick plastic. The whole thing resembled a darning mushroom with batteries housed in the stem.

7 Torch batteries however have a limited life. Used in case of emergency, two clear plastic hollow hemispheres coated inside with radium-impregnated paint, fused together into a ball, could be seen whichever way they fell.

8 Minature radios, complete with tiny earphones and a superb little 80 volt long-life battery, were housed in flat metal boxes commonly in use for packs of fifty cigarettes, or in tins disguised as lunch boxes.

simple, living clandestine lives in forests and caves. A resistance man continued to live and work at his normal everyday job, but was secretly loyal to the Allies. It was resistance workers who carried out damaging sabotage, train derailments, tampering with munitions and other acts to slow up the German war machine. They too faced death for their deeds, but they did have the satisfaction of a home life even if under occupation.

The S.O.E. was able to train and supply this secret army to a limited extent, and one of their functions was to assist the hard-pressed, constantly hunted *maquis* in the hills and forests and caves where they had their hidden quarters. It was the job of S.O.E. pilots to drop supplies of money, rations and arms to these fighters, and in many cases to officer and train them. My equipment was increasingly needed as this developed, and the telephone between my unknown S.O.E. contact and my office became busier by the day.

Each S.O.E. group was supposed to have its own radio operator, whose demands for batteries and other technical supplies never ceased. Codes were changed at random, with the need to supply ever more destructible paper of my flash or edible varieties. I had no connection with explosives (I think Major Clayton Hutton handled these), but money, clothing and all my secret gadgetry were in constant demand. Watches were especially valuable for the accurate timing of operations, and I was at great pains to ensure that those I delivered to S.O.E. (every one of them of Swiss manufacture, via my shadier suppliers) were of the highest possible quality and reliability. The fact that I still have mine, in perfect working order, suggests that I was well served by my traders in this area.

The Swiss have a genius for precision which not even the Japanese can match. I was fortunate in locating a Swiss lens-maker in Cornwall who was doing occasional under-cover work for the Royal Navy, making and polishing lenses for their submarine periscopes. I soon persuaded him to try his deft hand at producing minute lenses for some of my telescopes used by *maquis* and underground agents and supplied to them by S.O.E.

These actual telescopes had to measure no more than one and a half inches long. The diameter at their widest part of the barrel was no more than half an inch. The whole job was disguised and hidden in the S.O.E. agent's kit as a large cigarette holder, suitably stained with nicotine and tar. But the lenses so superbly made by my clever Swiss expert were a bare quarter of an inch in diameter, yet the telescope worked perfectly.

I suppose I should have realised that not only time-pieces, but alarm mechanisms, would become a much sought-after piece of S.O.E. equipment before too long. The need came down the phone to me in no uncertain terms one day. 'Can you get an alarm put in those watches of yours?' I was asked.

I thought it might prove impossible, but as usual said I'd get on to it right away and let my S.O.E. caller know. At first I tried one or two of my nefarious Swiss-dealers who came under the heading of 'enemy-traders'. No luck. Next I sought out a firm I had used before for obscure mechanical gadgets and timing mechanisms: Dreyfus Ltd. of Hatton Garden, London. There were two experts there I knew, and they suggested we had a meal together and discuss the problem in detail.

Over an excellent dinner at Percy's restaurant that evening – where I was interested to see Professor Joad, famous for his brilliance as a member of the B.B.C's radio 'Brains Trust' at a nearby table, tucking into his food and wine with great gusto – I put it to my hosts that they must produce not only an alarm mechanism which could be incorporated in a small, Swiss-made wrist-watch, but also one that would operate twice in succession. I had decided that this refinement was vitally necessary, since an exhausted agent might well drop off to sleep again after the first alarm. The experts made a number of diagrams on the backs of envelopes and nodded at one another hopefully. 'Leave it with us for a couple of days,' they said finally.

I did. And the model they came up with was absolutely right. It functioned perfectly at two-minute intervals. We used hundreds of them for S.O.E. and other work, and my absolute command that not one word of English of any sort should be left on any part was honoured to the hilt. I never heard of any user being suspected on this account.

The question of how to pay for these extra-curricular gadgets often bothered me. I was asking men, often in highly-paid and important positions in industry and commerce, to give me their time and expertise. Obviously the Ministry would pay in the ordinary manner for everything officially ordered; but how could I compensate for the effort and experience of the research and development of my requirements? Especially when not all such work was successful or rewarded by an order.

Waterlow, for example, deserved far more than they got for the excellent work they did for me. An S.O.E. agent often had to be dropped into France with literally millions of francs which he would distribute to the various underground groups. And when brand-new money had been made specially for this, great care had to be taken to prevent it looking as new as it really was. I did hear a rumour that Waterlow had their own way of getting over this difficulty. Their method for making new bank notes appear slightly worn with usage and agc was to have it danced upon immediately after being thoroughly dried.

I still find it hard to imagine the very dignified professional staff of that firm dancing around on a huge stack of newly counterfeited French francs, laid out indiscriminantly in loose piles on the floor. But perhaps they enjoyed their fandango, as much as I took pleasure in deceiving the enemy in other ways. It was all in a good cause.

I needn't add that it was equally important for their experts to ensure that the serial numbers of newly-printed money should avoid duplication. Due to the extreme professionalism of the Waterlow staff, few, if any, of our agents, to my knowledge were caught out.

This is not to suggest that Waterlow were the only firm of high repute taking extreme care with the making of my 'Q factors'. Any number of my suppliers were equally unselfish and unstinting in the consideration they gave to each item, however seemingly insignificant. Clothing manufacturers in particular, were taxed with a mass of delicate, often fastidious details.

For instance, French clothing had to be provided to suit a wide range of different classes and kinds of people, from farm-hands to priests and nuns. Shirts, underclothing and especially handkerchieves all had to be checked minutely to ensure that no British makers' marks or laundry labels remained on them. Genuine French tobacco had to go into the making of the black cigarettes customarily smoked. Even matches had to be minutely copied in order to perfect the exact type of striking material used on their small boxes. It was entirely different from anything used in this country.

In a store-room in London's Savile Row (actually, under the famous police station there) we kept a mass of equipment of all sorts, besides clothing. Our foreign cigarettes were made for us by the British American Tobacco Company, with no detectable difference from the real thing. They had only one snag. When kept for any length of time, the tobacco would dry and fall out. We then had to waste time replacing the stock with fresh supplies.

Also in the underground depot was a considerable arsenal of arms and munitions of all sorts, demolition explosives and so on, for use by S.O.E. and their resistance colleagues. All in all, it was a good thing no German bomb ever penetrated into its depths. An extremely able man, Naismith Shaw, was in charge of the supply and weapon depot. Fortunately for the agents, he was a man of fastidious and meticulous habits, highly organized and just right for S.O.E. at that time.

He must have had quite a time keeping a check on the strange assembly of real and fake equipment in his care. Our containers which were dropped into Europe often held many varied and weird contents. Several contained the personal shopping requirements of the agents. One S.O.E. woman even sent a request for Elizabeth Arden make-up, including the exact shade of lipstick and scent she preferred. I remember I had to make a special call on Elizabeth Arden to place the order. But wherever possible, if it helped to keep up morale, we sent what was requested. That meant supplying items like soap, chocolate, chewing-gum (for the Americans) and cigarettes. Cigarettes were not only invaluable morale boosters, they also were quite useful for carrying messages.

Very occasionally, the demands did become a shade bizarre. I particularly recall how one of our agents had got in touch with a resistance worker in a French clothing factory supplying the German Navy with underwear. This man excitedly told the agent that the vests passing through his hands were being worn by crews of U-boats. How could he sabotage them?

The answer came to the agent in a flash of near-genius: itching powder! We received his request for this with some surprise, but it was duly supplied in the next drop. I had it made up in well-sealed packs, so that there was no danger of any of the stuff escaping and giving our agent an irritating journey. I was later told that this man succeeded in sprinkling a liberal quantity on each vest he handled. In the tense hot atmosphere of a submerged submarine, I could well imagine that this could lead to unbearable friction. Indeed, it may not have been too far-fetched an idea after all. At least one German U-boat captain *did* surrender; he said he had been forced to surface and give himself up because of a mysterious epidemic which had swept through his men!

There were no end of these 'flea-bites' in our armoury of gadgets. If the itching-powder incident is anything to go by, some must have been at least as successful as far more expensive and dangerous equipment. My absence of knowledge of their value in use was, unfortunately, an occupational necessity: communications were too precious for expressions of esteem or gratitude. But we did learn from time to time how our stuff fared.

One way we did so was by carrier-pigeon. Special crates filled with these were parachuted gently down to our waiting agents and resistance forces. Many of the birds came flying home none the worse for their aerial 'lift'. And my plastic containers, I'm happy to say, stood up equally well. Fastened to the pigeons' legs they contained vital messages.

Years later, in the summer of 1979, I was to be strangely and deeply moved by a tribute to our humble work for S.O.E. and others behind enemy lines. I had taken my wife to have a look at Tempsford, where much of the wartime secret equipment used by S.O.E. was stored. The barn used as a quartermaster's store was still standing. Outside, on a simple board headed 'Tempsford, Gibraltar Farm', I read: 'Erected to commemorate the brave deeds of the men and women of every nationality who flew from this wartime airfield to the Forces of the Resistance in France, Norway, Holland and other countries during the years 1942 to 1945.

'The equipment for their dangerous missions was issued to them from this barn.'

To stand on that deserted airfield, remembering the courage and fortitude of those men and women, and to read these simple words commemorating their valour, was a thrilling and gratifying experience for me. Without their self-sacrifice, I told myself, we should now be living in an even wider desolation than that empty and disused old barn conveyed. In a real sense, I felt a part then of the strange, back-room war I had been engaged in.

I believe the whole area is now under grain; that is fitting. New life had been given its guarantee by these operations, as much as by any other. Yet the memorial to the courage of S.O.E., and in small measure to the work of supplying them, does still exist. Both the barn and its board have been removed and rebuilt at Duxford as an integral part of the Air Museum.

If and when the need ever again arises for such an enterprise, will we again find the resourcefulness, I wonder, the cunning and the enormous courage shown by these agents of World War Two?

10

FOOLS BY NIGHT

GROUP CAPTAIN PICKARD, the ace bomber-pilot who had found his way across the Channel using one of my compasses, was given the hazardous task of commanding the flights which dropped both S.O.E. and other agents into enemy-controlled territory and kept them supplied. He had a picked crew of night-fliers. The sorties they flew, under the most perilous conditions imaginable, were christened 'moon flights'.

I had my work cut out supplying these secret missions. Old R.A.F. hands had a saying: 'Birds and fools fly by day, only fools by night.' These lads, possessed of hawklike vision, brilliant combat records, and unparalleled courage, flew their sorties on nights of the brightest moonlight, prey to every sort of enemy attack.

What is more they flew in slow lumbering Lysanders. These strange grasshopper-like aeroplanes, developed by the Westland helicopter company, were justly known as 'old gentlemen's kites'. They were used extensively for army co-operation duty, spotting troop movements and gun positions. But they had one inestimable advantage for cloak-and-dagger work: no other aircraft in service at that time could land and take-off in such a small area; and none could beat the Lysander at standing almost still in mid-air.

So the moon-flyers were happy with their transport. And the nocturnal navigation aids we were able to provide them with helped, I'm proud to say, in keeping their casualty rates within acceptable limits. Most important were the landing lights laid out by our agents and resistance fighters to see them in. Skill and daring could get them to the drop zone, but only clear markings would indicate exactly which way to put down and take off again. Often with only a few minutes in between.

In Britain, we had needed no experience in such instant mobility. Even the most impromptu of our landing fields could be well-provided with a flare-path at short notice. One man in a small van with a number of goose-neck flares could set them out at intervals and these could be seen even in poor weather conditions, from a decent height. The only lights we could hope to provide for the secret agents, unless they were to be immediately spotted (as many were), rarely rose above the brightness of a pocket torch.

And if lights were vitally important, so too were the terrains chosen for the drops. Fortunately, we were able to rely on loyal farmers among the resistance workers, whose intimate knowledge of the countryside allowed our people the use of remote fields and areas unknown to the occupying force. Otherwise we should have fared far worse than we did.

At the start of the moon flight programme, R.A.F. pilots asked us to provide flares, or their equivalent, as a minimum landmark for their destination. Experience soon showed that these were not only impracticable but highly dangerous. We lost a number of agents and supply planes after lights had been spotted by enemy night patrols, and I was swiftly asked to develop a far less revealing form of landing light – preferably one which could be seen from the air and at extremely low altitude.

Obviously, low-powered, battery-operated lights buried in bucket-shaped holes were the answer. These could be covered over by day and only switched on, individually, as the time came near for the drop. In practice, many of the resistance men who used the lights learned to wait for the easily-recognisable sound of the Lysander's engine before risking ignition.

The torches provided by my suppliers (with whom I had discussed the problem in detail) were only good and effective at heights of up to a few hundred feet. Light from them was diffused by a mushroom-shaped top or dome of thick plastic, several times the diameter of the stem, where batteries were housed. The whole thing resembled a darning mushroom.

These had an additional advantage, in that they could be carried by women agents in with their darning wool and sewing materials. A later idea was to make the handle end of a bicycle pump into a torch. These not only looked like the real thing but functioned effectively *as* pumps too.

Pickard had one nasty experience, however, when the lights of the flare-path he was seeking became so dim that, by the time he flew over them, he missed them altogether and very nearly exhausted his precious return-fuel. Short-life batteries, indeed, had cost us more than one operation when badly needed agents were unable to be dropped, and others picked up. An idea to eliminate this awkward problem came to me one day while I was examining watches. The luminosity of their hands and figures had been increased at my request, to the point where they positively glowed in darkness. Would not a similar coating of radium-impregnated paint create sufficient light to be picked up by the keen eyes of a 'moon pilot', I wondered?

Inquiries inside my own Ministry produced the knowledge that all Britain's precious radium supplies were held in lead caissons, deeply buried in an area to the north of London, and well protected from any possible damage from air-raids. I shot off to see the scientist in charge, a Dr. Grove. After a keen discussion with this helpful man, I returned to London in some excitement. He had promised to try a variety of unorthodox experiments to see if it was possible to increase the brightness of the self-illuminating material to a point where it was still safe to handle but far more luminous. He had sounded far from pessimistic about the prospect. The main problem, he believed, lay in providing protection from radium burns.

Meanwhile I consulted other experts. Two clear plastic hollow hemispheres, it was suggested, could be fused together once the high-density radium had been painted onto the inner surfaces. This meant that they could be seen whichever way they fell. I urged my experts to press on, only to learn that no cement then in use was reliable enough for the delicate task of making the sphere thus formed sufficiently leak-free. Were we stymied, I wondered? Not a bit of it. By sheer good luck I was already dealing with another firm whose specialist technicians had recently been experimenting with an entirely new adhesive – virtually a breakthrough in the realm of such products. They tried it on my spheres; and the result, after test, was that the join proved stronger than the spheres themselves.

Telling myself that such good luck was not wholly undeserved, in view of the great self-sacrifice of our agents and resistance fighters, but grateful indeed to the fates which had sent me to these clever chemists, I gave them an immediate order. Nor did I forget them, as we shall see, when D-day preparations brought another urgent need for this magnificent adhesive. Meanwhile, the next problem was how to get the radium painted on to the inside of the plastic spheres without endangering the painters.

My earlier contact with the brothers Barker in Clerkenwell offered a possible solution, as they were used to painting luminous compass needles. I took a pair of spheres and some of the radium paint round to them to ask if they could handle it. As a double precaution the final product was wrapped in lead foil to ensure complete protection. The potency of the radium lasted for up to three months.

Any longer would have necessitated using an even stronger composition which would have been more dangerous to health. The brothers Barker did praiseworthy work for me on this and the country owes them a great debt. My radium supplier, Thorium, also deserves honourable mention. But then, so do so many.

Charles Pickard, who sent pilots out on these hazardous missions, was a most unorthodox leader. A giant blond Yorkshireman, he became quite a film star when he played the part of a bomber pilot in a popular war film *Target For Tonight*. But his real-life role was far more exacting than anything which could have been shown on the screen.

He had to invent stories to tell other R.A.F. pilots, who wondered what on earth these Lysanders of his were up to – painted black, as they were, and given special modifications (to allow them to carry the agents and their gear). The story Pickard gave out was that the planes and crews were operating photo-reconnaisance at night. This story held good, I believe, until one night a plane on its way back crashed in fog, killing everyone on board. Civilians removed the bodies from the crash before Pickard's men could get to it. The dead included two agents who were wearing the 'civvy' clothes I had provided. Obviously they had had nothing to do with photo-reconnaisance.

This started a chain of rumour and speculation. Bystanders began asking some very awkward questions. Pickard told them an inspired lie. The bodies, he said, were those of newspaper reporters who had been watching a raid on Germany from the air. When Fleet Street became more inquisitive, sensing a hot story, they were authoritatively told to 'shut up'. In wartime, this was an order.

Many of Pickard's men were almost as dare-devil as he was. One of them, Hugh Verity, became a model of what I earnestly believe was 'the perfect evader'. All fighting men (and women) were supposed to do their best to evade capture and, taken prisoner, to escape. Lectures were given to all crews before missions, stressing the best ways of carrying out a successful evasion.

Verity's concentration on these techniques was quite exceptional. He took every precaution possible. On every mission he flew, as one of Pickard's 'pick-up' pilots (for which he was awarded a double D.S.O. and D.F.C.) he wore under his service uniform a complete French civilian kit, provided from our store. He maintained that if he was ever forced to come down behind the lines, or found it impossible (as sometimes did happen) to lift his Lysander out of the mud to take off for a return journey, he would be able to transform himself into a French civilian and make his way home.

His battledress top, with its tell-tale wings and medal ribbons, would be speedily burnt. A Very pistol cartridge would provide ignition. In a locker of his Lysander (or 'Lizzie' as they came to be known) was a pair of French shoes, a beret and a complete escape kit – silk map, compass, French money and concentrated food tablets – ready for any emergency. Only his air-force blue sweater would be retained, since this could be mistaken for a civilian one. But all his clothes were scrupulously freed from makers' name tags and laundry marks. His papers, including a French passport with appropriate photograph and a false I.D. card, were kept up to date by regular consultation with his squadron Intelligence officer (who contacted M.I.9).

James McCairns was another of Pickard's boys who believed in being constantly and eternally 'escape minded'. Under his flying kit he wore Belgian clothing, having been helped back to Britain before he joined the moon-flight squadron by Belgian underground resistance forces. In fact, it was only due to this escape that he came to Pickard's notice. James Langley of M.I.9 happened to be in Gibraltar setting up a British escape organisation when McCairns made his way down there en route for England. Langley quickly spotted the young pilot as a perfect candidate for Pickard's 'air taxi service'.

Perhaps because he'd had an unpleasant taste of what evading an alert enemy could mean, McCairns thereafter took extraordinary precautions: more even than Hugh Verity. His fountain pen, I learnt, squirted tear gas. He also carried a hidden .38 revolver. His clothes were a mass of hidden escape implements. Ironically, he lost his life in peacetime, in a flying accident.

Eccentricity was not at all out of place in Pickard's squadron. One of his ace flyers disappeared, returning several days later having learned how to fly a captured German Junkers 88. He had also been fitted out with one of my German uniforms, my German cigarettes and other equipment. The plan was for him to fly in with other German night fighters and land on a Luftwaffe station, take over a modern Junkers 88 night fighter, and then fly to England with it – complete with a new form of radar which was puzzling our experts at the time. Before he went into this risky operation, our air boffins fortunately got the information with less risk and drama.

Aircraft, of course, were far too precious to be risked on foolhardy ventures, and nobody knew better than Charles Pickard how vital to Britain's success in the war was the preservation of his 'Lizzies'. He had to make the decision, often on scant information, in every case where a plane was required to fly to an unknown destination, land in enemy territory and return intact with its precious complement of agents and crew. He came to rely, I like to think, on the landing lights and other gadgets I supplied, and never refused a mission where conditions made it possible.

Fortunately, too, the supply of Britain's front-line planes was increasing rapidly under the demanding hand of Canadian newspaper tycoon Max Beaverbrook, backed by his friend Winston Churchill. Under him was a most remarkable man. Wilfred Freeman (or to give him his full title, Air Chief Marshall Sir Wilfred Rhodes Freeman, Bt.) made a massive contribution to our ultimate victory in my opinion, one that I am sure Beaverbrook, as Minister of Aircraft Production, recognised fully.

A pioneer of aviation in the First World War, he forced through production of the Lancaster heavy bomber, the pathfinding Mosquito and eventually Whittle's jet engine – all against strong and conservative technical objections and advice. It was to men like Freeman and Pickard, with vision and daring in equal parts, that this country owes so much of its survival. I recall Lord Hives of Rolls Royce saying about Freeman: 'Without (his) foresight and imagination, no efforts in 1940 (the Battle of Britain) would have yielded results.' I would go further: without men like him the war would have lasted much longer.

The Americans, too, owe much to Freeman for his development of the Packard Rolls Royce Merlin engine. At Schweinfurt, on October 14, 1943, 198 American bombers had been destroyed or damaged, out of 291 sent. To counteract these appalling losses the Mustang fighter, with an Allison engine, had been rushed into immediate production. Fortunately Freeman's persuasion finally convinced the Americans to change to the Merlin, with phenomenally successful results. The Merlin/Mustang concept saved endless aircrew lives and thousands of bombers.

In my own sector, the need to think up gadgets which might be needed was paramount. I had to develop a chess-player's genius for thinking ahead correctly. With the black-out threatening every after-dark activity, I turned my thoughts repeatedly to the problems of illumination, both in escape and evasion. Nothing is riskier than to have to show a naked light in a totally dark area. Yet, since much ground could be made at night a need existed to study the contours and directions of my mini-maps, which could seldom enjoy the luxury of being more than handkerchief-sized and often were no bigger than a playing card. How to give illumination sources to those using them, without at the same time making them an obvious target for the German patrols, was a problem I wrestled with continuously. Then, one day, the answer presented itself quite accidentally.

I was on one of my 'shopping sprees' in the West-end, peering into obscure shop windows to see if anything displayed there might make a useful addition to my gallery of gadgets. My eye was caught, in the same window where I had first spotted a Gigli saw, by a thin tiny bulb used (I was told on excitedly entering the shop) by surgeons for delicate internal investigations during their operations. I was delighted to find that, attached to a small flat battery which I had specially made, it could be held in the cupped palm of the hand over a map without any light showing. Someone a few yards away, at night, would be unable to see a single shaft or glow of light. The ideal object! I immediately placed an order for a whole batch of them, and saw that they were included in escape kits wherever possible.

Pickard and his moon-flight crews were among the first to receive any of my gadgets which could lessen the dangers of their missions. My S.O.E. contact would listen to me whenever I told him I had had a brainwave, and more often than not I would find myself having to supply a gadget I might only have vaguely imagined while having my bath (a regulation four inches of water only, in those days of rationed fuel). Under ordinary circumstances, I might have boxed a bit more clever, holding back until I had developed each notion to the point where I could speak with assurance of its capability. But the S.O.E. venture was so obviously in need of every possible assistance, I passed on anything that came into my head, and took the rest on trust.

So, to an extent, did the men drafted to Tempsford

(and prior to that to Tangmere and other air stations from which the early S.O.E. sorties were flown). One young pilot later told me how he'd first arrived at the secret base and been astonished by its appearance. To begin with it didn't look like an R.A.F. airfield at all. Camouflaged by Maskelyne's magic into an imitation of a busy farm, with genuine tractors in the fields and yards, it gave him the uneasy suspicion that he had been the victim of a squadron leg-pull.

Gradually my informant's trained eye detected runways stretching through the cabbage fields, and some of the large grain-storage buildings, he saw, had suspiciously well-oiled, hangar-like doors. It was still daylight, and no aircraft could be seen; but one of the rustic-looking farmhouses became, as he entered it, too obviously an officer's mess to allow for any further doubt. This was a station all right, but what sort?

Two unusual points about the mess soon added to the mystery: the food was better than he'd been used to (Pickard had leaned heavily on R.A.F. catering command to provide the finest fare available in rationed Britain). And the other pilots, gathered round the bar, were all seasoned men, with well above the average number of 'gong' ribbons under their wings. Nobody talked about flying, or what the squadron's duties were which could command such a select complement. He was left with the impression that he'd been sent to a rest camp for veteran flyers, who had completed a series of 'ops'.

There was, however, something particularly strange about the place. He found he couldn't use the telephone. He wanted to put a call through to his girl-friend and family, to tell them he'd arrived at his posting 'somewhere in England'. Not to say where you were was regulation procedure in wartime. But not to be able to use a phone at all was most odd. Where on earth had he landed up?

Next morning, he was asked to see the C.O. Having muddied his shoes crossing a couple of farm yards from his quarters, and passed by a duck-pond with live ducks quacking enthusiastically, he came to the cow-shed where he'd been directed. Pushing open the door he found an alert guard, armed to the teeth. He was ushered through into a completely modern, and extremely well equipped Control Centre. A massive map of Europe dominated a room in which W.A.A.F. and R.A.F. plotters were moving models with push-rods and pointers, while radios and teleprinters hummed in the background. A burly R.A.F. policeman escorted him to an office clearly marked 'C.O.', knocked, then held open the door for him.

Inside, the atmosphere was relaxed and informal, but highly charged. The final surprise was still to come. When he'd been told something of the moon-flyer's role in the secret war, the C.O. turned to personal details of his life from which it was clear that M.I.5 had carried out an intensive check. 'Perhaps you could help us with one or two more details?' the C.O. murmured. Peering at the pilot's file in his hand, he asked: 'Tell me, this girl-friend of yours ... is she a brunette?'

My pilot friend could only guess that the C.O. was pulling his leg. 'No sir, she's a redhead actually,' he said. 'Ah, that explains it.' The C.O. sounded relieved. 'You see, somebody told our chaps that she's a red – and he must have thought it meant politically! I'm afraid we can't be too careful.'

As part of normal moon-flight squadron procedure, it explains much about their unorthodox commander Charles Pickard who flew over 100 missions himself. He risked his own life on numerous occasions to take S.O.E. and other agents into enemy territory. He picked up and dropped urgently-needed supplies well behind the lines. His photo-reconnaisance work over Bruneval was our chief source of information in making the models which the commandos studied before the raid. He was in all ways a most exceptional commanding officer.

And security was his watchword: no pilot or airman at Tempsford was allowed to discuss his work, not even among colleagues. The rules were explicit and the Germans never once tracked the moon-flyers to their lair though they searched long and hard for this vital base. They never came near to realising that their aerial photographs of a rural scene, which could have been painted by Constable, in fact showed plainly one of the most extraordinary and effective centres of Britain's secret war effort.

As the chief correspondent of the German Transocean News agency in occupied Paris, Georg Schroeder, wrote: 'The British have special arms factories for making weapons for their own agents. From England, automatic pistols (some of my 300?!) are dropped, along with ... a whole vast range of special weapons.' They felt the sting of them, but finding them was another matter.

11

B.B.C. CALLING

IN 1941, soon after America was jolted into the war by the Japanese assault on Pearl Harbour, President Roosevelt sent a most interesting Christmas present to King George VI. At first glance it was a small, pocket-sized camera. But if the shutter button were pressed, music or talk from a radio broadcast was heard in place of the familiar click. The object was a brilliantly conceived miniature wireless set, with volume and tuning controlled from the two film-winding spools, and a perfectly adequate loudspeaker set in the lens.

I had been ferreting around for a midget radio, easily dismantled and hidden, to send to our escape committees in the P.O.W. camps, and for other purposes. Nothing I'd seen on this side of the Atlantic came anywhere near this in portability, size or performance. I straightaway asked for half a dozen similar to be sent over for detailed examination, and was gratified to have them land on my desk – still freezing cold from the flight over in the bomb-bay of a Flying Fortress – only days later.

By this time I had established a number of useful, enthusiastic contacts with radio manufacturers and technicians. I shot round to one of them in a pool car, carrying the tiny set in a briefcase. Their chief expert was as fascinated as I was. He explained that to make anything as small he would have to try and reproduce the mini-valves which the Americans had managed to incorporate. I told him to go ahead at full speed.

Another problem was the case. The camera disguise was an amusing coffee-table gimmick, but hardly likely to be of use to us. It was also far heavier and bulkier than was necessary to hold the tiny parts of the radio. I left it to my trusted expert to find a more suitable slim-line casing, and to make our own facsimile of the U.S. model.

Naturally, I was impatient. The provision of radio to our captive forces was as important as any activity I was connected with, simply because it could, with the magnificent help of the B.B.C., destroy the distorting and defeatist propaganda poured into our prisoners' ears by Hitler's propaganda minister, Dr. Goebbels. This all too often carried shreds of truth to establish confidence, then added viciously false accounts of British and Allied losses and disasters.

Fake English newspapers were printed by the Germans to reinforce this purpose, then left about in the prison camps. Only when some of our chaps who had been in the printing trade saw that the ink on these was still wet, did the ruse fail. But without the B.B.C. bulletins, a prisoner was less likely to remain escape-minded and it is sad to recall that a few gave their parole – a promise not to try to escape – for this reason. They thought the war was lost.

I was determined to use the gift-radios to prove that it was far from being so. Also, by ensuring that a supply of dismantled sets flowed into the camps hidden in musical instruments and games – which this miniature would make possible – I knew that we could pass coded messages over the air for receipt by the escape committees monitoring them. In every way this could become one of our most effective tools.

So far as the set itself was concerned, I hadn't too long to wait. The technicians working on the valves perfected tiny models of the normal light-bulb-sized objects, and I was shown that they were 100 per cent effective in use. Minute earphones were developed by another firm, and I was able to congratulate my contact on having done a first-class job 'for my Ministry' which – as he well knew, having been sworn to secrecy and told something of the reason for this assignment – was never to be seen by the Ministry of Supply at all. The trouble was, as he explained to me, that the set would have to rely mainly on batteries and no adequate 'mini batteries' existed at that time. Most wartime sets used huge affairs the size of a two-pound box of chocolates and twice as heavy. Some even needed wet-cell models as well, housed in pint-sized glass jars. Such small batteries as there were – for torches and suchlike – had only an extremely limited life.

Having got so far I refused to be defeated without the very dickens of a struggle. Surely, I reasoned, there had to be wizards of electricity who could come up with a solution? There was a firm I knew from past experience whose chief technician could do most things. But unfortunately my previous encounter with various directors of this company had been far from satisfactory. They'd shown a distinct lack of enthusiasm, to say the least, and I'd put them on my mental blacklist as a result. However, in desperation, I now decided to forget the past and called in at their office. The same directors greeted me, and I told them what was required. What was more, I laid it on pretty thick: this was a vital job, urgently needed to supply our front-line forces and so on. The war depended on their efforts.

Earlier experience had shown how necessary this attitude was. I had asked them to make a long-life battery for my landing lights. A short time after this, one director rang me up to say that it was simply 'not feasible'. This was, I later discovered, a despicably self-centred evasion to prevent their having to turn any of their profit-making machinery over to my work. I found this out when I insisted on visiting the company personally to learn all the details, because the bosses had continued to be pessimistic about the whole scheme and I had asked to talk directly to their technical people. Eventually – and perhaps because it was nearly lunchtime and they wanted to clear me out of the office – they reluctantly agreed. They rang down on the internal telephone for their ace technical man to join us immediately. The fellow came in, wearing a white coat, and was introduced to me. Before he could be asked, or told, what was required of him by his employers, I jumped in with the crucial questions.

'Is it possible for you to make a pocket-sized battery with a long life?'

The man was startled into an immediate reply. 'Certainly, sir,' he said. I had then a glimpse of some flushed and angry faces.

I paid little attention to what else was said after that. The technical manager soon left us, to return to urgent work downstairs. I turned to the directors with a 'well, that's settled then' expression on my face. They had the good grace to look sheepish as I faced them with an order for an immediate 1000. 'I want them to give a guaranteed longevity of three times that of an ordinary torch battery,' I said as casually as possible. 'After all, that is what I understand your technical people are able to provide.'

The directors looked extremely uncomfortable because this didn't suit their book at all. At length, one of them – the one who had telephoned me – said hesitantly: 'Well, yes, I suppose we'll have to do it. But for God's sake don't let on to the Board of Trade, will you? If these things of yours ever got on to the regular market we'd lose a fortune. Don't you see – customers would need only one of those batteries in place of three ordinary ones. And they cost about the same!'

I'm afraid I showed very little sympathy for such open-handed self-interest. 'My job is not with the Board of

Trade or any other organisation,' I said. 'You just make my batteries, and go on making them whenever I ask you to. Your firm's commercial problems are not my pigeon at all. Good day to you both.' And I marked the official order I sent off to them by special messenger that night 'Delivery within one week'. It was the beginning of a business association of which I believe the directors were, in time, unjustly proud. I believe they ended the war not only wealthier, but one was also decorated for his 'work on behalf of the war effort.' In fact it was solely due to the technician's efforts that I had got long-life batteries at all.

My reception, now that I approached them a second time, was altogether different. They produced a superb little 80-volt battery for the radios. Flat cells were fitted together in series, giving ample power for radio reception if not transmission. It meant that B.B.C. and other vital information could constantly reach our prisoners and underground allies. The truth would get through.

Sometimes, I believe, Signals geniuses among the P.O.W.s managed to adapt the power circuits of the sets to work on electric current from an ordinary light socket. This was far more dangerous, since it was difficult to conceal it in the time between an alarm and the arrival of inspecting snoopers. So our batteries became firm favourites, if only for this reason.

But my fury over the earlier lack of co-operation of those directors who, but for my persistence, would have got out of taking any part in my secret production, is still with me today; one black mark in an otherwise glowing picture of selfless and unstinting help from my suppliers.

The problem of containers for the sets was meanwhile being fully investigated. I solved it eventually, as I did so many others, by using an everyday object which fitted the job perfectly. In this case it was a flat metal box then commonly in use for packs of fifty cigarettes. Our minute valves, and other components of the 'Q radios' could just be accommodated in one of these, with the earphones and batteries tucked away separately. The aerial was in the lid. But to improve reception a longer aerial could be made from the metal-cored twine used to tie Red Cross parcels. This was the one instance where we allowed ourselves to tamper with these parcels, though only on the outside, and in a way which could hardly be considered conclusive evidence of escape activity, since the twine could equally well have been the proper material for the purpose.

I heard much later that they were passed without question by the German guards, who seemed innocently pleased that the parcels were now being more securely tied together, never suspecting the true purpose of the twine.

I might add that there were many instances where the men themselves, using fair means and foul, managed to provide radio receivers for themselves. One escape committee, I heard, obtained a working radio receiver from a local German by bribery, threat, and blackmail. I've no doubt there were many similar instances, but this one I can vouch for.

One of the P.O.W.s at the camp had a job as an assistant to a German joiner or carpenter. This man, he discovered, secretly kept a small radio-receiver at his home. He used it to listen in to foreign broadcasts, a crime punishable by sentence to a concentration camp. By pretending to sympathise with this weakness, the P.O.W. assistant soon got himself into the German's confidence. In exchange for tobacco which the joiner brought him, he would give him regular supplies of chocolate, coffee and soap, items of wartime luxury which the average German rarely saw but which the Red Cross parcels provided for our P.O.W.s.

These, of course, were allocated by the escape committee. They kept up the supplies for some time, then set the trap which had all along been the purpose of the exercise. One morning the assistant arrived at work with a long face. 'I'm in terrible trouble,' he explained to the joiner. 'They've found out that I've been stealing supplies from our store to give to you. And they've made me confess who I've given them to.'

The joiner, who had been supplying his wife and twenty one year old daughter with all these luxuries, (to the point where the daughter had written a letter to the P.O.W. requesting certain types of chocolate) saw the danger at once. If the Camp Commandant got to hear of the barter he had been receiving, the Gestapo would be informed and his life would hang by a thread. The least he could expect would be transfer to a labour battalion. 'Is there any way we can square the British Commandant?' he asked. 'Surely he doesn't want to turn you in for such a thing?'

The P.O.W. kept him dangling while pretending to negotiate. Eventually, he came in great relief to the joiner with the news that the Commandant would take the matter no further on one proviso. The joiner must let the P.O.W.s have his portable short-wave radio receiver. If he refused, then the whole matter would be put to the German command under the heading of 'fraternising' – a crime punishable by death.

Delighted, the joiner brought the dismantled set to work with him, piece by piece, day by day, and the assistant took it back to the escape committee hidden in his lunch box. It was carefully re-assembled by wireless operators at the British camp in the workshop where they were supposed to be making electric detonators for German gun batteries. Thereafter they provided the camp's first clear reception of the B.B.C. from London.

Prisoners were not lucky enough – nor were we – to live in an age of transistors and miniaturisation. These bulky sets were as near as they could come to effective communication with the homeland often at enormous risk to those who listened. But, to hear the truth, any risk was worthwhile.

In Burma, I have since learnt, British captives forced to work on the building of the Burma Road lost many lives and suffered greatly from the attempts made to retain radio links with home. On one occasion, during a long march to a jungle building-site, one secret British radio hidden in an accordion fell heavily into a ditch when its player was roughly handled by a Japanese guard. Through the instrument's squeeze-box, a revealing collection of wires suddenly made their appearance. Only the greatest good luck saved the accordionist from immediate bayonetting.

In Burma, too, batteries for hidden radios were stolen at enormous risk from Japanese trucks. While diversions were mounted to occupy the drivers, good batteries were swapped for old duds used up by the P.O.W.s. Sometimes, the new ones had to be hidden in dixies of hot rice, the prisoners' only food.

Radio communication was one of the most vital factors of the secret 'Q' war. We had tried several miniaturised models before the Roosevelt gift came into our hands, but with limited success. One we had sent over to agents was housed in a sandwich box. This had been made to look like a workman's lunch. It usually escaped notice, but on one tragic occasion one of these caused the arrest of two of our finest and bravest operators.

Yvonne Rodelatt, code-named 'Jacqueline', was the first woman S.O.E. agent sent into France. She and 'Pierre Leclerc', as we called her companion (his real name was Pierre Culioli), had been fully trained by S.O.E. for the mission and equipped with one of the early miniature radio sets. A grandmother of forty-seven, this remarkable woman had undergone every sort of rigorous preparation, including a parachute course. I still find it sad to think that one of my gadgets unmasked her and her accomplice.

But not initially. By the time she was caught, Jacqueline had achieved the destruction of the Chaingy power station, as well as the blowing up of the Bronzavia factory at Blois, which manufactured components for the *Luftwaffe*. With others she had destroyed over 200 key electricity pylons. Locomotives and their sheds had been blown up, and serious derailments accomplished of German troop trains. In fact, so many German officers and men had been killed and wounded in these wrecking operations that S.S. Colonel Mersch considered her area, Sologne, contained 'the most dangerous resistance workers anywhere in France.' In June 1943, he had ordered in specialist units of the S.S. to deal with the menace of this one woman.

Yet Jacqueline remained free. And would have done so, but for the radio. She and Pierre were driving down a lonely road with two Canadian S.O.E. agents. They were taking them to a safe house when they found themselves halted by a German roadblock. The S.S. officer in charge had no reason to be suspicious. He found nothing wrong with Pierre's or Jacqueline's papers. These simply showed them to be a forestry official and his middle-aged wife. But the two newly-arrived S.O.E. agents in the back seat were uneasy and their fear communicated itself. The officer turned back to Pierre. He noticed for the first time the small tin lunch-box on the seat between him and Jacqueline.

'What have you got in the box, there?' he asked.

Pierre smiled. 'Sausage,' he said easily. 'And not so good, but there's a war on you know!'

One of the agents in the back lit a cigarette. His hand holding the match – one of mine, a careful British reproduction – trembled a little. The S.S. officer's eyes narrowed.

'Is that so?' he said. 'Well, perhaps I'd better have a look. You and your wife, get out!'

To Pierre and Jacqueline, the tone of voice, and the order, meant only one thing. The game was up. They exchanged a glance of silent agreement: she may even have whispered an urgent 'allez!', but that I can't swear to. One of the Canadians who escaped death with them brought us the rest of the tale.

Pierre simply put his foot hard down on the accelerator. The car tore through a crude barrier of oil-drums set up by the patrol. As machine-gun bullets ripped into the tyres, he and Jacqueline zigzagged to a halt. The S.S. officer followed them breathlessly. Wrenching open the door, he picked up the lunch box and opened it. 'So,' he said heavily. 'A sausage, eh? Well, I think this will be sufficient to end your need for sausages for ever, don't you, Monsieur?' It was. Jacqueline died in the gas chambers of Belsen a fortnight before the Allies arrived. Pierre survived the notorious Buchenwald camp. An equal blow to us was the loss of one of our secrets, the radio. The Germans took it apart and copied the brilliant way our experts had managed to create such a small, and effective, instrument.

The Roosevelt Christmas gift nevertheless was of the utmost value. It really was a brilliant triumph of reduction technology, at that time in its early infancy. We had some three and a half thousand airmen as well as many other servicemen in the prison camps, all badly needing encouragement as well as supplies and information, to forge a workable escape. The F.D.R. radios played an almost irreplaceable part in this. Compasses could be made, maps could be copied, and special clothing faked up by camp tailors and others. But radio parts simply had to be imported, or obtained, from outside. And that was where my small operation came in.

12

ON THE RUN

THERE WAS LITTLE OF strategic military significance in my work, though I like to think that it may have been useful to military commanders. Supplying, occasionally thinking up, gadgets and equipment of benefit to our secret agents and resistance fighters, or of help to escaping P.O.W.s and shot-down aircrews evading capture, was a Lilliputian enterprise compared to the great deeds of the war.

Mine was a very personal war effort. I had to see in the mind's eye the conditions experienced, or likely to be, by the people I was working for – the men and women in the field – and relate to them. When an agent dropped by parachute, or was landed from a motor torpedo boat or submarine, in a land bristling with an alert enemy, nothing could be left to chance. For that reason I had to rack my brains to cover in advance every tell-tale clue which could give our interlopers away.

Nothing could be too small or too insignificant. Shreds of English tobacco lodged in the seams of jacket pockets, even the bristles of a shaving brush from an animal foreign to that country, all such details were important, even before we began kitting our people out with secret, concealed tools of escape and manoeuvre. I had to think hard and long about every single strand of fabric and piece of material before passing it on to the various departments I was serving.

The basic evader's kit evolved, for this reason, in a constantly-changing pattern as more and more ingenious gadgets came into being. In its final composition it contained a tube of Nestlé's full-cream enriched milk, a small saw, concentrated food tablets, maps, compasses, full-cream chocolate, water-purification tablets, miniature matches, elastic-strip bandaging, needle-and-thread and benzedrine tablets. Aircrew were instructed in the best use of these simple instruments of survival and movement.

They also knew and delighted in the clever wheeze we had thought up to convert their easily identifiable fur-lined flying-boots into ordinary looking shoes. A tiny knife was hidden in the leather. With this a grounded airman could cut off the upper part, leaving a well-formed pair of shoes which could have laces fashioned from the stitching at the ankle. By reversing the severed leggings so that the sheepskin became the outside, and using the needle-and-thread in the evader's kit, the airman could tailor himself a warm and simple-looking waistcoat not unlike that worn by many shepherds. (If interrogated, he could always imply that it had been taken from a crashed airman on his farm.)

The plastic container of the evader's kit could be used as a water-bottle. The stopper too was a 'Q factor' item: I had arranged for a small compass and watch to be secreted in it.

Food, needless to say, was of the greatest importance to any form of escape, evasion or undercover activity. Men on the run cannot get far on an empty belly, and the need to eat and drink has given more absconders away than anything else. I made it my number one priority for this reason, despite the more glamorous attractions of secret compasses, saws and other sophisticated mechanisms.

Milk, condensed and fattened to the maximum, was one of the hardest substances to pack in a form which would not sour or dry up. I had gone into the question of its packaging with both M.I.9 and my S.O.E. contact, and they favoured a small octagonal tin. I had a sample made by Metal Box Ltd, the firm which makes any number of canned food containers in this country. But at Nestlé, the suppliers of the concentrated milk, the director I dealt with, Mr. R.S. Worth, was appalled at the idea of filling such awkward receptacles. He, of course, had no idea to what use they were to be put. I realised too that with eight nasty corners there would be considerable waste when sucking this concentrated food out of the tin.

I had to think again. The departments demanding the kits were pressing me to get on with them, so there was no time to waste. But if small tins could not be filled without altering the entire process used by one of our major firms, what could take their place? The answer came to me next morning as I brushed my teeth: a squeezable tube.

Instantly, I popped the half-finished toothpaste tube into my official brief case and made my way to the office in high excitement. A call to Nestlé put me in touch with Worth (and a colleague of his, another of the firm's directors who had become interested in the project, a Mr. W.S. Crocker). We met later that day.

Before their amused gazes, I produced my toothpaste and asked if they could adapt it to hold their concentrate. It took a few moments for the idea to sink in, but before I left both these experienced men were in their shirt sleeves adapting and adjusting machinery to accept the tubes. I was in no doubt about the result.

A snag, however, was in sight. 'You'll never get the tubes produced in this country,' Mr. Worth told me mournfully. 'We have the dickens of a job getting even our standard tins.' I suspected he was right. With the canning industry's skeleton labour force already tied down with high priority work, it was extremely likely that I would find it difficult if not impossible to obtain anything as sophisticated as my tubes from any of them.

But this put me on my mettle. Now I knew that Nestlé could fill the tubes, once I had provided them, I had taken too good a step towards achievement to be put off. 'Hold everything,' I told Worth. 'I'll get back to you as soon as possible.' In fact, it took me exactly twenty-four hours to persuade a reluctant toothpaste-tube manufacturer to supply my needs. As so often happened, the man himself finally promised to work as late as was necessary to ensure that my quota – which had to be turned out after the main defence work of the day had been completed – reached me in time. He was typical of many.

In some jubilation, I rang my Nestlé directors with the news. The first 100 tubes would be in their hands the following day: could they fill them immediately? Mr. Worth, on the other end of the line, sounded completely flabbergasted. 'Never known a government official move so rapidly!' he commented. I was able to explain that I wasn't really a government body at all – just a farmer who was quite used to moving quickly when weather conditions called for it. He took the point.

So began the flow of tubed, condensed, high cream-enriched milk. Included in their escape kits, it became a familiar part of the diet of evading aircrews on the run from enemy patrols and doubtful French farmers. If I may judge from the number of orders for these vital items, they were an enormous success. Both M.I.9 and S.O.E. pressed me for more and more of them. I still possess one of the first batch, made in 1942. Whether or not they still contain the nutrition they had nearly forty years ago I cannot say, but at least my tube is still soft and certainly it has not yet exploded.

Nestlé and the tube-makers between them produced literally millions of these items. Before long we adapted them to fit into a corner of the escape kit, by squeezing them into oblongs. The idea was later adopted by the Americans, and produced commercially after the war. It is odd to think that prior to that moment when, toothbrush at the ready, I looked in my shaving-mirror and saw the tube in my hand, nobody had apparently ever thought of using such a container for foodstuffs.

I grew used to strange requests from my various departments. But in the second year of the war a call reached me from Commander Philip Rhodes who, apart from handling Naval Intelligence at M.I.6, was also a versatile liaison between that department and M.I.9. It was about ten in the morning of an extremely hectic day when his call came through, and I recognised him instantly, without any need for the coded exchange we went through as a matter of elementary caution. His requests were always unusual; this one was remarkable.

'We need 100 cubes of potato powder,' he told me. 'They must be delivered here within twenty-four hours. All right?'

It was anything but all right. However, I never argued with a request, or denied its possibility until I had vainly tried every feasible method of satisfying it. This was a real snorter.

On ringing a director of the Ministry of Food, I was told – as I expected to be – that no such thing as potato powder existed, and it could not be made. Recalling that we had once used dehydrated vegetables for soup, I asked if there was any dehydrated potato in the country. 'We might try Chivers, the jam people,' I was told. 'I believe they've been experimenting with something on those lines. They might have a small quantity ready.' 'Right, I've got twenty-four hours to get it made up into one inch cubes,' I said. 'Ring them right away to put all they can aboard the guard's van on the next train to London. Then ring me back with the time of its arrival. I'll have a dispatch rider waiting to collect it.' I still had no idea how it could be cubed, but that was my head-ache.

By extreme good luck I'd just had dealings with one of the wizards of the cosmetic industry, Mr. Bather, the chief chemist at Coty's. He had been putting solid fuel and other things into cubes for me, items like dried vegetables, tea and so forth. I went round to see him and told him about my potato powder. The problem intrigued him and I left with his assurance that he'd do his best to solve it – if I sent the stuff round to him right away. It was due to be delivered at four o'clock; so he had until nine a.m. the next day to come up with a solution.

I was still in my office at ten that evening when the phone rang. Coty's chemist was having difficulty, he said, in finding a suitable, edible component to make the powder stick together. I urged him to press on. Then I offered up a small prayer as the minutes ticked by. At midnight, he rang again. A component had come to light, he said, that would do the trick. But after half an hour the potato powder started to swell up. The cube expanded and cracked.

More urgings and encouragement ensued. By four a.m. he had solved the problem. By nine a.m. the 100 cubes were completed and delivered, exactly within the specified twenty-four hours. I never did discover what he used to make them stick together, but I have looked on ladies' nail-varnish with suspicion ever since.

The powder itself was a novelty in those days. Both the chemist and I took some home. We found it made a good thickener for soup, but wasn't too wonderful as mashed potatoes (though later improvements made it palatable). I was amused to hear that, after the war, some of our stocks were sent to Dartmoor Prison. Food was still short and real potatoes temporarily on ration. But when my 'secret formula' was served to the convicts it nearly caused a riot! The prisoners at Dartmoor must have been somewhat pampered, I feel. Though perhaps it is significant that I never received another order for that particular product.

On all secret operations, quality and space-saving were absolutely top priorities. Food such as tea leaves, dehydrated meat, and vegetables could all be pressed into tight cubes, and my chief chemist friend, Mr. Bather, did a great deal of research for me on these. I wonder sometimes if my interest in this form of nutrient compression has brushed off on my farmer son, Brian, who was among the first in Britain to turn freshly-cut grass into highly concentrated, enriched cubes at his North Devon farm. I was seeking concentrations of the most highly nutritious foods such as nuts, raisins, oatmeal and honey. Compressed into bars, any of these could be life-savers to escaping men. Chocolate, a favourite and handy food, was especially studied at my request to increase its food value to the maximum. I well knew how sustaining it could be, from personal experience when, as a young man, I was all-but penniless travelling in Italy. I had pretty well lived on it.

An Austrian scientist and food specialist sent some to me at the office one day. It was magnificent. A rich chocolate containing fruit extracts, rum and various liqueurs. I knew that such a delectable addition to our evader's kit would be unlikely to stand the test of time, since these had to be issued to, and carried by, all aircrew on missions over enemy held territory. So I reluctantly declined.

Nestlé's produced for me a chocolate with the maximum food value. As they explained, cocoa powder itself has no food value; so it had been eliminated. Only the cocoa bean-oil, or butter, is nutritious. Thus the bar was white and anaemic-looking. Unfortunately, its taste was flat and seemed synthetic, though actually it was the essence of pure chocolate. Since I could not possibly risk producing an adverse psychological effect in anyone who ate it, it had to be dropped.

For the French resistance and the maquis I had the

French *Menier* chocolate made and dropped by air with their regular supplies. Here again I insisted on increased nutritional value, but with a rather surprising result. Having persuaded the Ministry of Food at Colwyn Bay to deliver a consignment of their precious concentrated full cream to my suppliers for the purpose, I received a call from Menier's director to say that it had 'produced too light a colour'. My suggestion – that they dye the chocolate to make it look like the real thing – was greeted with astonishment; but they did, and it did. I have a slab of it still, in its simulated French wrapper.

Swiss chocolate, certainly one of the best if not *the* best in the world, contained 35 per cent fat. The special Menier chocolate I had made contained 45 per cent. Those who were sustained by it while making their way to safety, or escaping from P.O.W. camps, will know that it was worth its weight in gold. They owe much to the men who pioneered the magnificent Swiss chocolate industry: Francois-Loìs Cailler and Philippe Suchard, followed by Kohler, Peter, Tobler and Lindt. But Swiss chocolate only became world famous with Henri Nestlé, who first invented condensed milk, and it was this firm which perfected my best product, often stretching their severely restricted supplies to the limit to do so.

My Austrian scientist, who had made the too succulent rum chocolate, managed to bring his own manufacturing process and machinery with him when he fled from Hitler. So we had the use of this, and took full advantage of it. While the Germans were using ingenious chemicals to produce *ersatz* confections of all sorts, we could make the real thing. Unfortunately for our agents, this could not be supplied to them for fear of its origin being discovered. We had to make a deliberately *ersatz,* and much poorer, quality for their consumption.

There was no end to the search for concentrates. It might seem rather ordinary nowadays but some of the items we came up with back in the early days of the war were quite startling, even to those very resourceful men who did the conjuring tricks after I had saddled them with various projects. For instance vitamins were urgently needed as an anti-scurvy measure. A concentrate of orange-juice was the obvious answer, but getting it made in those days was a tiresome exercise. First, we had to obtain the oranges, at a time when the tonnage of our merchant ships being sunk by U-boats was alarmingly high. We relied on fruit from Spain and Portugal, but on occasion were glad to receive supplies from the Argentine. We then had to devise a method of reducing the orange to powdered form without losing its nutritional value. I'm happy to say that we, and the many clever people who assisted us, were so successful that I believe our methods are still, in more refined form, in use today.

Similarly, we managed to perfect dehydrated food tablets which did not take up too much room. The best I can say for them is that they were better than nothing. When thrown into hot water, they produced an unappetising, but nutritious, soup of sorts. Then there were tea-cubes, which were equally uninteresting but useful. But the most popular were the Horlicks Malted Milk Tablets in our kits. These had very high protein food content – being concentrated sugar with glucose, malt and condensed milk – yet tasted really rather good. Compressed raisins and nut tablets were excellent to chew, too.

Speedy purification of water was another essential for our men on the run. At first we supplied conventional tablets of halazone, a perfect sterilizing substance, but these took too long to act. We needed something quick as well as effective, so I put the problem to a colleague who promised early results. One day he appeared in my office in great excitement. He had discovered an entirely new chemical which he swore would do the trick.

I might add that even though my office was fully

secured, all papers locked away and that sort of thing, it was still rather dicey for civilians such as my suppliers to wander in off the street and ask to see me. There were times during the war when this did occur and there was only one thing to be done to preserve my 'cover' while keeping the visitor's nose out of my real business. I would sit the chap down, explain that he was not exactly in a simple Ministry of Supply office, and before he knew what we were about he would be sworn under the Official Secrets Act. He was then, as I was, barred for thirty years from revealing any hint of our proceedings on pain of death. Many a surprised face has left my office under those circumstances.

In this case, the fellow just showed up. I'd mentioned on the telephone that I was too busy to go over and see him for a while, and his enthusiasm couldn't be contained. Since I didn't know if or when it would recur I let him demonstrate his discovery.

He'd brought a bottle filled with water. One glance showed me that it was full of obvious contamination; muddy, with lots of little bits of debris floating around, which wouldn't settle down even after we waited ten minutes. He shook the bottle up again and then added his secret formula. In less than two minutes all the muck had settled to the bottom and the water was absolutely clear. It was a perfect conjuring trick, almost a miracle.

Needless to say we got him into production immediately. But to this day I don't know what the formula was. He kept that to himself. So well, in fact, that I believe he went into commercial production with it after the war.

I had, of course, taken a look at ordinary water filters well before this. They were useless for our needs; heavy, porous, earthenware things. As an alternative, I had tentatively managed to arrange for the manufacture of lightweight plastic jobs. But these proved too slow. The miracle chemical was far better, and a great boon to men who risked, at the very least, a severe bout of gripe from drinking any untreated water supply, especially in North Africa. (In our escape kits for the aircrews involved in desert warfare I included purifying tablets so that they could drink their own urine.)

As a farmer, I was always particularly alive to the needs for food in our operations. Napoleon's wise belief, that an army marches on its stomach, was equally true of men on the run. The trouble was getting the food to them.

From 1941 to 1943 our shipping losses were at their heaviest. In the Mediterranean we relied on Malta alone as the rallying port for our supply route. We were losing nearly 80 per cent of convoys, and that little island was under constant attack by the Germans and Italians. Hundreds of war planes and a goodly part of the Italian surface and submarine fleets were committed to its obliteration, which both Hitler and Mussolini had sworn to accomplish.

So, when the North African landings were in prospect (as I realised from the maps I was handling for escape kits and S.O.E.), I began to think about my years in Morocco and Algiers. We had had phenomenal success in increasing our food yield. If something on the same lines could be worked out to reduce our invading army's dependence on imported food, shipping would be freed for other duties.

Why, I wondered, could not local Arabs be persuaded to grow the food for us? With the right approach, I felt sure that Arab farmers would co-operate. Especially if we provided them with seed, and a proper sowing and planting programme.

But first I had to sell the idea to the war lords. I used my red telephone, the 'hotline' to the War Cabinet. After an engaging chat with a Miss Cox who was one of the War Cabinet Office's senior administrators, I was asked to go and see her. I then outlined my plan, convincing her that where Arabs and farming were concerned, I knew what I was talking about. Not only could we send over vegetable seeds and seed potatoes, I explained, but the B.B.C. could back us up with instructive talks and appeals to the Arabs, by radio, setting out ideal planting times, correct fertilisers and so on, using phosphates from their own extensive mines.

Miss Cox's reaction to all this was highly gratifying. Though untutored in the ways of the Arabs, she immediately recognised the merits of my scheme. Would I, she asked, mind explaining it once more to a group of 'experts' (she had the grace to smile when using that particular word) from the Ministry of Food and Agriculture? Not a bit, I told her. A few days later I was called round for a conference of what appeared to be a sub-committee of the War Cabinet specially set up to go into my plan's possibilities. Three dozen earnest people, mostly unknown to me, apart from Miss Cox and an official called Mathews of the Food and Agriculture Ministry, listened to my notion in silence. They then questioned me as to the types of food I had in mind, sources of seeds, growing times – matters I had already worked out well in advance of the conference.

Thank you very much, they said. The meeting was over. I'd no way of knowing whether they had approved or not, so I assumed the worst. But a few days later I had a call from Miss Cox telling me the scheme was on. I was to be closely involved with it, in addition to my other duties. I gave a silent cheer, since this was truly work after my own heart.

A crop of potatoes and vegetables could be grown in ten weeks. I decided it would be expedient, knowing Arab farmers' mentality, to provide not only for the American and British troops but also for their own requirements. A large tonnage of seed potatoes was therefore shipped at my request from Britain, while seeds for the other crops were flown in from America in the bomb-racks of war planes. I was to handle the propaganda side of the scheme personally.

Broadcasting over the B.B.C. to instill the right attitude, as well as methods, into North African farmers takes a certain knowledge of psychology. We did not want the Germans saying 'listen to that Englishman spouting all that rubbish.' At the same time, the farmers had to be wooed into action. I asked the B.B.C. to line up three Arabs from the Moroccan Embassy. They read my prepared script which would tell the truth as we knew it to my farmer friends along the 2000-mile coastline bordering the Mediterranean. It baldly stated that the time had come when we would drive Hitler and his Nazis from their lands, and they could help us to do so. 'God and Allah', I reminded them, 'help those who help themselves.'

I went on to encourage them to dig and plough to the last ounce of their strength. Food, I cried, is a weapon in war, more important than guns. No army can move without it. No country can exist without it. As these were farmers I was talking to, I laid it on, not with a trowel, but with a two-furrowed plough.

'For two years the Nazis have robbed your lands of food and sent it to their own country,' I wrote. 'While, in consequence, you and your families are facing hunger. In England we have a slogan: "Dig for Victory." Make this your slogan too. We are sending you large quantities of seed potatoes and vegetable seeds. These will be unloaded on your own shores, for you to plant and sow. Start at once to prepare the soil: In the name of Allah, "Dig for Victory!" '

Such broadcasts were followed by expert run-downs on the seasonal problems of cultivating crops in the area. Technical instructions on the latest and best means of weeding and hoeing were backed by pep-talks on increasing food production. None of this was ostensibly for an invading force, but that was not necessary. Once grown we could tell them how to store the crops. And here Malta's experience under siege helped immeasurably. The Maltese had learned to use every available bit of soil, growing 'short crops' and living for long periods on dried pumpkin, potatoes, and goatmeat. They had also been very successful in storing their pumpkins and potatoes. So we adapted their methods to North African conditions, and broadcast these to the Arabs.

All this was viewed by some of my colleagues with thinly-veiled suspicion. What was that strange chap Fraser-Smith up to now? In my first radio script I'd used the biblical adjuration: 'Go to the ant, thou sluggard, and consider her ways.' The Ministry of Information thought it unwise, so I asked for an interview with the Chief to discuss this.* It seemed to them that we were offering the Germans an easy propaganda weapon with which to win Arab favour. They would say that the fanatical British were trying to convert the Arabs to the English Bible – an affront to Islam! I explained that one of the prophets of the Koran is Solomon, and I knew that this quotation from the Book of Solomon would go down extremely well with them. The M.O.I. shook their heads in doubt, but finally let me go ahead.

All this was well out of my normal line of course. But it did seem worthwhile. We saved some shipping. The troops got fresh food. And the Arabs were pleased with us, because we'd encouraged them to be self-supporting. It shows what a rather mixed-up group of experiences can produce when put to work on a single project.

My Moroccan farming, the Malta storage experience, a strong B.B.C. overseas service and some rather heavy-

* Imagine my delight on entering his office to find the 'Chief' was Kenneth Grubb (later Sir Kenneth Grubb). I had met him in 1925 to discuss non-professional missionary work before going to Morocco, and again in 1935 in Madrid at the first Protestant Congress allowed in Spain.

handed but quite sincere messages of inspiration, all tossed into a plan which was basically just common-sense. But when one remembers the story told of the First World War – when sandbags needed in the desert were reputedly sent by sea from Europe, filled with sand – the need for this commodity can be fully appreciated.

13

SPILLSBURY'S BODY

ORDERS WERE NOW coming in on my telephones at an increasing pace, both in scope and sophistication. It was no surprise to be asked by M.I.6, one day in the early winter of 1943, for a water-tight metal container more than six feet in length and, as I realised later, large enough to hold a body. I'd been supplying almost identical containers to S.O.E. for some time, to be used as hold-alls for guns and ammunition dropped by parachute to our underground shadow-forces in occupied territories, including the French maquis. I took this one as a normal request.

Certainly no hint was given me of its real purpose. Nor did I discover, until very much later, how close to its development was a neighbour of mine, the great forensic scientist Sir Bernard Spillsbury who, as Home Office pathologist, had unravelled so many baffling and gory murder mysteries in his time.

The canister was to be exactly six feet two inches long, about three feet in width and to weigh somewhere in the region of 200 pounds dead-weight (I should perhaps have suspected something from the use of that phrase). At the time, I had never heard of Lt. Commander Ewan Montagu, the master of 'dirty tricks' who had conceived the plan.

It was, as I subsequently discovered, brilliantly simple, and extremely effective in mystifying, if not completely fooling, the Germans. The corpse of a man in British uniform was to be put into the sea off Spain, where currents would cast it up on the shore. In papers left on the body were detailed plans for an invasion of Sardinia which was, like the plans, a complete fiction. The 'man who never was' (as the corpse, code-named 'Martin', became known subsequently) was to put our enemies off the scent of the *real* Allied invasion planned for Sicily.

'Martin' was to be selected from among recent victims of pneumonia by Sir Bernard, and preserved in my container packed in dry ice until the time came for his journey onto the Spanish beach. Poor Martin; hardly a holiday visit to those sunny shores.

The dimensions were a bit unusual, I thought. But the idea of housing a body – even though I was instructed to provide a valve and vacuum pump to the air and water-tight container – never seriously occurred to me. The cover markings were also different from any I had used before. When I managed to raise a mildly curious question about them I was curtly told that the whole operation was 'for a floating weather station.' Had I thought about this more carefully, I might have doubted if this could be so, since no metereological results of any value could be hoped for from any such a device.

Even when I was told to include a 'Mae West' lifejacket with the canister, I failed to grasp the purpose of it. It seemed to me that if anyone was foolish enough to try to gain weather statistics from a floating tin-can, then probably there was a need for some expert to risk his neck in the ocean setting it up. Hence the need for a lifebelt.

Spillsbury could have put me right. He had been my neighbour for over twenty years, in my younger days. Now that my family and I were again living in Croxley Green we met fairly regularly. My family home was almost opposite to his, and we often acknowledged one another on the platform of our local railway station where I would come across him from time to time deep in the columns of his newspaper. He was a tall man, with a deceptive mildness of manner. Studious eyes behind pebble-thick spectacles, and a rather disarming addiction to the old-fashioned wing-collar; these characteristics stamped him as someone from a past generation, perhaps a retired gentleman visiting his London club to discuss the conduct of the war from the depths of an armchair. How far he was from any such backwater image we now know.

The story of his work on 'the man who never was' came to me later, well after the war. It did not surprise me. But our mutual interest in the 'Martin' project was a complete revelation. Spillsbury apparently took the greatest pains to ensure that the body would stand up to any forensic tests the Germans cared to apply. At first, our Intelligence chaps had held back details of the scheme even from him. He insisted on knowing where the corpse would land. As he explained – and this was a measure of the man – if it had to be put ashore in Germany the condition of the lungs would have to be different from that of a body washed up in the Mediterranean. He was grudgingly let into the secret and immediately went to work.

For this reason a victim of advanced pneumonia was used. Only in such a case would the water in the lungs correspond to salt water from the sea.

A pity Spillsbury and I could not have spent those often delayed and weary wartime journeys up to London discussing these interesting problems together; but nothing could have been less likely. We remained mere nodding acquaintances until the end, and I very much doubt if Sir Bernard ever knew of his neighbour's interest in the drama.

A man I did know, though only slightly, was Ian Fleming, creator of the legendary secret agent, James Bond. The reason I well remember him is that he used – or misused, rather – one of my most imaginative little gadgets, a golf-ball which contained a compass. Fleming, who had liaison contact with M.I.6 next door in Broadway, was officially a personal assistant to Admiral John Godfrey, the Naval Intelligence Department chief in the early part of the war. Godfrey, I gather, thought a great deal of Fleming. Commodore Rushbrooke, his successor who took over in November 1942, is said to have taken a much dimmer view of the great spy novelist. I hope that wasn't because he had tried to play golf with Fleming's fictitious 'Q-balls', because that would have been disastrous.

The whole point about the secret ball, usually sent out to our P.O.W. officers in a box of six, all sparkling new (as a suggested pastime for their long sojourns), was that they had to perform *as* golf-balls. In other words, they had to bounce with the same vitality and elasticity as any top-flight ball ever made. Fleming's contraptions, as described so fascinatingly in his novel *Diamonds Are Forever,* wouldn't have fooled an Irish farmhand let alone the lynx-eyed prison officers and S.S. of the *Oflags.*

Their hollowed-out centres, he believed, would act equally well for diamonds as for compasses. Ingenious, but totally inadequate. Had any suspicious investigator tried to bounce Fleming's balls they would have given their carrier away instantly. They would simply not have performed as golf-balls.

Ours, on the other hand, had the very considerable advantage of an appropriately designed rubbery interior (as shown in exhaustive tests by the makers before offering them to me) so that they would bounce down any fairway with as much spring to them as a normal ball. That was the difference between fact and fiction, I'm pleased to say. So far as I know, not one of our 'Q balls' was ever detected by the Germans. Fleming, I fear, would have stood to lose many of his best agents with his.

But I mustn't be uncharitable. Fleming, I'm told, was always keen on my gadgets. I heard in a roundabout way that his interest extended to trying them out on other members of the Naval Intelligence staff. How he managed to prise them loose from Ridley or Rhodes I really can't imagine, but he was known to have great charm and persuasive powers as well as a highly-tuned imagination.

He certainly put this to use, though not always with the effect intended. I had a hand in one of his more ingenious schemes which came to nothing. His plan was to make use of a serviceable German bomber (we had by then managed to obtain quite a few of these in working order) as a means of getting hold of a German Naval Intelligence code book.

The scheme Fleming proposed – and almost put into operation – involved flying the German plane back towards Germany with a *real* enemy bomber force, returning from a raid of some British target. The 'Q plane' would then apparently get into difficulties, with fireworks ignited on the wings and fuselage, to give the appearance of flames. It would come down in the Channel, close to the German gun positions on the French coast. And a German air-sea rescue launch would, Fleming assumed (no doubt correctly), be put out at once to take off the crew. Fleming's specially-trained commandos hidden aboard the bomber would then overpower them and seize their code book intact.

I was brought into this exploit at a fairly early stage. My task was to provide German uniforms for the commandos to wear on the raid. Fleming, ever a dramatist at heart, was leaving nothing to chance. He insisted that the 'Trojan Horse' bomber crew should be dressed correctly for the part. So I set to work, in what was now becoming a routine manner for me, to obtain the necessary kit and equipment.

There is always one small but extremely awkward problem in a major job of this sort. Here it turned out to be the *Luftwaffe* cap badge or 'rondelle', as it is known in the trade. It was made from an unusual type of synthetic which had a unique texture and blend of colours. Any copy which was not absolutely accurate would be detected immediately. Unfortunately the synthetic material used was only manufactured in Czechoslovakia.

I was using textile experts from Courtaulds, the fabric people, and even they were baffled by this small badge. There was no way they could guarantee our copy against detection, I was gloomily informed, unless we had the assistance of one of the Czechs behind the original design. 'Well,' I told them, 'perhaps that can be arranged.'

I used my red telephone. Could M.I.5 come up with any Czech textile expert capable of helping us over this hurdle? They could, I gathered. In my turn, I was told to leave the matter in their hands. A Czech expert they found gave me the secret and a firm in Leek, Staffordshire, made the rondelle. How they did it I've no idea; but the complete uniforms came through precisely on time. They were beautifully made replicas, if anything rather better tailored than the genuine article, but undetectable as fakes to the most expert eye and touch.

Unfortunately this only made it doubly disappointing when I was promptly informed that the whole operation had been scrapped. I don't doubt that Fleming was furious. What nobody had told him was that we *already* knew the German Naval Intelligence code – thanks to the remarkable Enigma and Ultra de-coding machines, whose existence was one of the best kept secrets of World War Two – even in Intelligence circles!

My efforts, however, were not wasted. There was a constant demand for German uniforms of all types and sizes and for all manner of secret missions. Often the work we put into copying enemy equipment produced unexpectedly valuable results for our own side. I was once presented with a new model life-jacket just issued to the *Luftwaffe*. A hundred exact replicas of it were required immediately, I was told. This should have been no problem: we'd made dozens of similar life-belts in the past.

Only this one had an interesting addition, a small metal bottle fixed to the outside of the jacket. It was, I discovered, filled with compressed air which could at the press of a button be released to inflate the jacket once the wearer had landed in the sea.

Our standard life-jackets had to be blown up by mouth, and quite often a ditched flier was too exhausted to be able to do it satisfactorily. As soon as we had reported its usefulness, the German device was swiftly incorporated in our own Mae Wests.

There was also a strange appendage to the life-jacket itself: a waterproof bag of what felt to me like powder. I was asked to find out what it was. Very gingerly, I opened it. It seemed harmless enough, so I had the bag resealed and sent for analysis. But, without realising it, I had got some of the powder on my fingers. When I next went to wash my hands, to my astonishment the water turned a greenish yellow colour and became instantly fluorescent.

I saw at once what this meant. A man floating in the sea could release the powder which would spread over a wide area and be readily spotted by air sea rescue patrols. Needless to say, this was another invention which our Air Ministry was delighted to take up.

As soon as we got into production, I gave Spirella House of Letchworth the task of making the life-jacket and filling the bag, while I.C.I.'s famous chemists reproduced the powder. Unfortunately the girl set apart to do the latter so spoilt her clothing that special Ministerial machinery had to be set in motion to obtain extra clothing coupons for her!

Rather more hazardous, in that I had to risk being suspected of unpatriotic activities as a result, was the occasional use I made of shady merchants and dealers. Some supplies urgently needed for our agents had no substitute. These were sometimes quite unobtainable outside enemy territory. I therefore had to resort, with severe misgivings, to odd individuals who were – though I lacked absolute proof of the fact – obviously, and quite illegally, trading with the enemy.

One day I received a telephone request to call at M.I. Headquarters. On arriving I was informed that two mysterious men would like an interview with me in room 321. Before going I enquired whether my Chief had sanctioned the interview. He had.

The men said they were from a security section and were investigating a leakage. The head of the Trading with the Enemy Department had reported that a director of a fairly well-known firm, who was one of my suppliers, had shown him a secret object. He felt it should not under any circumstances have been displayed. Security therefore had interviewed the firm's director, who admitted that he had shown it, but would make no further explanation because of the Official Secrets Act. His advice to them had been to contact me.

I told them that the director had done, and was doing, first-class work for the Ministry. He had considerable European knowledge and, with ministerial permission, had obtained invaluable materials from enemy-occupied territory for us. I said I would investigate this specific case and report back.

I discovered that a whole year had passed since this director had shown the secret object to the chief of the Trading with the Enemy Department. The chief had apparently been in the position to help get the material to make the object, and the director had appealed to him to do so, believing that a man in such a high position was safe to confide in. Unfortunately he and the chief had subsequently fallen out over another matter entirely, and after a stormy scene had barely been on speaking terms ever since.

I satisfied myself that the 'object' (a shaving brush) had been placed on my obsolete list since all this had occurred, as its particular function had been suspected by our enemies and I had been forced to withdraw it. The chief of Trading with the Enemy would not have known this fact, of course; but he should have realised that much can happen in twelve months in wartime. Perhaps peevishness following his row with the director had played its part. Men in important positions can be smaller-minded at times than their inferiors. They tend to forget that the chief of a government department can be far easier to replace than the director of a firm with invaluable specialised knowledge. My contact may have been wrong in speaking to a senior civil servant as he did, but I had no wish to lose him from my list.

Shaving brushes with secret compartments gave me more than one headache. The main problem was that bristles are taken from whatever animal's hair provides the easiest and best source of supply. Local animals were therefore used almost exclusively in their manufacture, and their coats differ remarkably in texture and type. To avoid detection by the enemy, it was vital for me to get hold of the exact hair.

For quite a while I was foxed by German brushes, when it came to supplying our agents working in that country. All my experts were tried in turn. 'Tell me where these bristles come from,' I requested in each case. But nobody came up with a positive answer until one bright chap hit on the unlikely solution that the Germans, short of native bristles, were using very fine Russian hair in their brushes. To get hold of a supply of this was far from easy, in spite of our alliance with the hard-pressed Soviets. In the end I managed to trace a supplier in Argentina, where more than one of my 'enemy-trading' contacts had their businesses.

One of our main difficulties in dealing with requests for 'Q' items from P.O.W. camps, via M.I.9, was in sorting out genuine from false messages. Those helping the escape committes could be infiltrated, we were only too well aware. False requests for my 'Q' items could threaten the lives of all future users. We had to be on our toes to detect any suspicious order which might lead to secrets being revealed, and this meant keeping fully up to date and in regular contact with the camps themselves.

This wasn't easy. Code systems were, of course, used between camps and M.I.9 for information exchanges, but these could also become known to the enemy. The only safe way was for our own man to act as a courier, and in at least one case known to me a man, specially trained by M.I.9, was deliberately set adrift in a rubber dinghy wearing R.A.F. flying-kit with the express purpose of being taken prisoner by the Germans.

Once inside a P.O.W. camp, this man made his true identity known to the delighted escape committee leader. And with the knowledge he gained in the camp he was able to make a successful escape and bring back to M.I.9 a great deal of useful data.

14

HESS AND TREACHERY

BUT WHAT WERE THE enemy doing all this time? How successfully did we deal with their gadgets and secret devices? Responsibility for security against agents operating in Britain rested entirely on the shoulders of M.I.5, with whom I had little contact. I knew, however, that they were fully in control of the situation. In fact, they had dealt with many of the German spies sent over here, putting them in the bag at the start of the war. I therefore assumed that the tricks the Germans used were not always as efficient as ours.

They, of course, had no corps of determined resistance fighters and underground insurrectionists to help them. The few crypto-fascists in Britain, fanatical members of Oswald Mosley's blackshirts and others who sought a Nazi victory, had been rounded up and detained for the duration.

Yet M.I.5 were certainly not prepared for their biggest coup. On May 10, 1941, Rudolph Hess, Hitler's deputy, landed in Scotland. Why he did so, what his motives were is still in doubt. What I and others in Intelligence knew was that here was a major enemy figure who had dropped, voluntarily, into our hands. Every scrap of information we could obtain from him was likely to be of the utmost value.

Hess was Hitler's right-hand man. Though the Führer disowned him publicly when it was realised that the scheme had misfired, there is little doubt in my mind that it was planned from the top. Hess's mind was not deranged as some people liked to believe. He came to the Duke of Hamilton, with whom he had had some previous acquaintance, mistakenly convinced, I am sure, that Britain would accept him as an emissary and that the threat of Russian communism to the West would bring our two nations together.

My part in the mystery was rather less direct. I had already heard of Hess's astonishing visit over the B.B.C. when my telephone rang. I cannot now be absolutely sure of the sequence of events, but I remember the note of excitement in my caller's voice. 'This is M.I.5,' he told me, 'We'd like you to copy a very senior German officer's uniform for us. Could you be at our office here tomorrow evening at eleven o'clock?'

'Wouldn't it be simpler to have the uniform sent round to me, so that I can show it to my tailoring people?' I asked.

' 'Fraid that won't be possible,' my contact said impatiently. 'We'll only have it for a few hours. You'd better arrange to bring your chaps along with you, if that's necessary.'

It certainly was necessary. I was no more able to cut and tailor a uniform than I would have been to blow up Hitler's bunker single-handed – much as I would have liked to do the latter. I immediately rang up my contacts at Courtaulds, and they arranged for one of their most senior textile wizards to come over to M.I.5 with me. His job would be to identify the exact material and, if possible, to supply it.

We had already had ample experience with German army and air force officers' kit. So we knew the type of materials used in their manufacture. This was for a very senior officer, I explained. It was therefore possible that it might differ from more lowly kinds, as the vain Reichmarshal Goering's personally designed and elaborate uniforms differed.

I then called S.O.E. and asked if they could rustle up one of their finest and fastest secret tailors. This they readily agreed to do. It was not the first time I had made use of their people on a *quid pro quo* basis. In the 'civil service war' between M.I.6 and the fairly recently-formed S.O.E., I often had the feeling of being the rope in a tug-of-war. But I think I had managed to convey my support for both these organisations in a way that did not upset either of them, or add to the unfortunate (and to my mind petty) friction between them.

The next evening, I took my party along with me in a M.I.6 car. The three of us were ushered into a bare room with a plain table and very little else that I remember. On it, laid out as for a dress parade, was the immaculate uniform of an officer in the *Luftwaffe.* It was obvious that this belonged to someone in a senior administrative capacity, or a political bigwig. It still did not strike me, until one of the M.I.5 people present took me aside and whispered in my ear, that it was Hess's.

'Get your chaps to buck up,' he told me sternly. 'We've given Hess something to ensure that he doesn't wake up until morning. But this is his uniform, and we must have it back to him in the next four hours.'

Nobody mentioned to me that Hess was then an honoured guest in the Tower of London. If his uniform was to be returned by first light, there was certainly no time to be lost. I urged on my experts. First, the Courtaulds man examined the material the tunic and breeches were made of. He nodded. 'This is a high quality synthetic light-weight gabardine,' he announced. From a bag he produced a swatch of similar fabrics of different colours and held one against the tunic. It matched perfectly.

'Feel this,' he said. I took Hess's tunic between forefinger and thumb with, I must admit, a most unaccountable feeling of excitement. There was something surrealist about handling the uniform of a man who, second to Adolf

Hitler himself, had led the German people against us in the bloodiest war of our history. I thought of him lying asleep in his well-guarded bed, unaware of what we were here to do. Then I pushed the more romantic aspects of the event to the back of my mind and got on with the job.

'Well?' I queried. 'I agree that that is the cloth. But can you supply it in the quantity we want? And at once?'

My Courtaulds man nodded cheerfully. 'Enough for a small army if you want it,' he said. 'You're lucky on this one, we have it in stock.'

I went over to the table and passed my hands through the various pockets, feeling for false seams and hidden compartments such as we inserted in our senior officers' uniforms. The buttons were standard issue, I ascertained, unlikely to yield any gadgets such as were hidden in ours. Finally, I had to admit that if Hess had carried 'Q-factors' in normal life, he had discarded them to come and visit us. I turned to my tailoring cutter.

'All yours,' I told him. 'Take the measurements you require. And please avoid doing anything to the uniform which could be noticed by its wearer. It has to be returned exactly as it is now.' To neither my Courtaulds friend nor the tailor did I, or the M.I.5 people present, say one word about Rudolf Hess. Whether they guessed the identity of the uniform's owner, I cannot say.

The copy was duly made and delivered, though not to me. What it was used for – *if* it was used – is something I should be interested to know one day. As usual, no explanation was given. I sometimes wonder if we intended sending somebody back in the copied outfit to try to penetrate the Nazi high command. If so, it was a most daring notion, whether or not it became impracticable later on as the Hess saga developed. The risk of having a double – what the Germans might call a *doppelganger* – occupying the role of deputy to our leading antagonist would almost have been worth a man's life.

German agents who came to Britain were quite often caught and turned into double-agents by M.I.5, so that they could return to Germany working surreptitiously for us. But Hess could hardly have been expected to do that. Some of the others who came over were picked up quickly, showing the results of very sloppy training before leaving Germany. One walked into a pub at nine a.m. and asked for a beer, with no apparent knowledge of British licensing hours. Another tried to take a train. When asked for the fare of 'ten and six', he handed the booking clerk ten pounds and six shillings! Off he went to a prison camp.

I have no doubt we also made stupid mistakes. Some of our S.O.E. operatives walked straight into the hands of the Gestapo. Unfortunately, it was often difficult if not impossible for us to discover where they had blundered. My view was that it was usually due to betrayal rather than staff failure, or lack of preparedness. I devoutly hope that it was that, and not my secret equipment, which was at fault.

But we did learn about some of our failures. I was mystified once to hear of a man in a German P.O.W. camp reporting that he had received nothing at all from home. We knew that his wife had been sending regular supplies of precious rationed goods and comforts to him. When he managed to get a message to us, we checked up and found that a man she described as 'terribly sweet' had been calling on her. His trick had been to persuade her that he was an expert at getting the packages to the camps more quickly and efficiently than by the normal route. She had been parting confidently with several of these before we caught him. No doubt he'd been getting fat prices for the goods on the black market.

I also had to cope with the occasional unenthusiastic supplier, such as the battery firm mentioned earlier. These were rare, I'm happy to say; but I did find one or two people who put their profits before the country's needs. There were also those who played with the truth to wriggle away from my Ministerial requests – despite the fact that, in wartime, these were in the nature of commands backed by full governmental and defence regulations. A tobacco firm put up a really disgusting show in this way, which still infuriates me.

I had had repeated orders from S.O.E. for genuine Balkan tobacco for their Yugoslavian section, working with Marshal Tito's hard-pressed partisans. None of my contacts had been able to find any among their stocks, and I had met with a blank turn-down from each of them in turn. Then one morning, when I had more or less reached the end of this particular road, I had a telephone call. Though on this occasion, the caller was a woman it was strikingly similar to the call I had received while searching for the 'gallant 300' automatics, mentioned earlier.

This lady explained how she had come by my number, which the other caller had not. She was, she said, secretary to a senior man in another department who 'dealt a lot' with me, so she knew of my search for exotic tobacco. Would I like to know, she asked, where some of the material I was so vainly seeking could be found? She had information of interest, she said.

When I had assured myself that this was no hoax (her use of a certain code word used by the department she was connected with soon convinced me) I was delighted to give her my word that there was nothing I should appreciate more. She thereupon mentioned the name of a firm, a maker of popular cigarettes, which she claimed was holding a secret stock of Balkan tobacco in store against the time when they could use it to cash in. As I had impressed on their senior directors the great and urgent need for this, there was no possible excuse for such evasion. My blood boiled at the thought of their behaviour, should it prove to be true.

'Where exactly is it?' I asked my caller.

'Not just in one place,' she told me. 'They've got it

hidden all over England. In a dozen different locations. What they're planning is to wait until the end of the war and then produce it, as if they'd just managed to import it from overseas.'

I thought hard. Then I said: 'I must thank you very much indeed for this information. You may have done this country a great service by telling me. I shall act immediately, if you'll just give me an address where the tobacco is hidden.'

'I'll tell you that with pleasure,' she said. 'But why not go for them all? I can let you have a whole list.' And this incredible woman rattled off a long list of addresses of depots and warehouses in remote districts of Britain. How she came by it I did not inquire. But when I put down the receiver, my P.A. girl asked if I was feeling all right. I was humming a happy tune.

'I'm fine,' I told her. 'And I'll be even better in a few minutes time, when I've spoken to Scotland Yard. Get them for me, would you please?'

That was not the last occasion for happiness over the matter of the Balkan tobacco. Police visits discovered the exact amounts my telephone caller had described to me. It was all confiscated and delivered to the partisan forces by S.O.E. and, I was told, went a long way towards upholding morale among those desperately hunted and beleagured men and women of Tito's ragged army. The directors of the company which had deliberately held back in spite of my order received the worst stinker of a letter I was capable of writing. It made my day.

Treachery was never far from my thoughts, in view of the risk our agents ran once the Germans discovered how the 'Q factors' worked. As S.O.E. activities extended into other areas I was faced with an increasingly complex 'shopping list' which made security all the harder. In Holland, out of 144 Dutch secret agents landed or dropped, only 28 survived, which gives an idea of the vulnerability of some theatres, and the need for extreme caution in equipping secret infiltrators.

Gadgets I regarded as highly sensitive had to be most carefully issued for this reason. The Dutch were immensely brave and determined in their resistance to the Germans – nobody more so than their gallant Queen Wilhelmina – but inevitably there were traitors.

The trouble was that the Dutch government in exile in London was largely composed of fossilised refugees from the Dutch East Indies, suffering in many cases from colonial phobia and greedy personal ambition. So much bickering went on that the head of British Secret Service, Holland Section, once lost his temper and asked their War Cabinet if, after fighting each other so incessantly, they had 'any time left to fight the Germans'? The point was well made. We had little doubt that many of our efforts to supply and assist their underground forces went astray through nothing more than this administration's weaknesses.

There were, also, far too many cases where Gestapo bribery in occupied Holland bought information at a terrible price. It is impossible to say how many brave Dutchmen perished as a result, or how much of my work was discovered by the Germans. I prefer to remember the ones that got away: in this case, far too few but, in at least one outstanding case, a moving tribute is due to what native cunning, courage and skill could do with the help of the few 'tools' I was able to provide. The man who showed all these qualities in a most magnificent escape from the Germans was Dr. Lipmann Kessel.

Kessel, a surgeon and a Jew, was captured at Arnhem during the British airborne battle for the bridge. With another Dutch doctor, he was put in charge of the Elizabeth Dutch Hospital behind the German lines. They were allowed to treat and operate on hundreds of wounded Allied soldiers and some of the Dutch civilians injured in the fighting. Kessel had hidden one of my mini-radio receivers in his medical equipment.

He set it up, surreptitiously, in the operating theatre, reckoning correctly that no German would penetrate this sterilised area. He also knew that the murmur of the B.B.C. news bulletins could not be detected above the clatter of instruments, the gurgle and hiss of blood-pumps and gas cylinders. With the news coming in this way, he was able to cheer many of the desperately depressed and wounded soldiers in his care, who knew only that their own gallant operation had been a failure.

He did more. Against the advice of German physicians working in the hospital wards (one of whom recommended euthenasia for all serious wounds) he carried out brilliant and delicate surgery on men whose lives hung by a thread. His success astonished even the arrogant Nazi doctors whose prisoner he was. And, while he worked, often taking only snatches of sleep between exhausting four-hour bouts in the theatre, he managed to make contact with the local Dutch resistance. They advised him where 'safe houses' were to be found in the countryside, and how to pass on men fit enough to walk to the escape routes already established and used by shot-down airmen. With their help he sent many lightly wounded soldiers back to Britain.

At first, the resistance insisted he send only single men, one at a time. But one day a message was passed to Kessel as he was removing shell splinters from a badly wounded Parachute Brigade sergeant. 'Send four,' the message, crudely written on toilet-paper, read. 'Tonight.'

Lipmann Kessel finished the operation with his usual care, tying the minute knots in the stitches which were admired by all who saw them. Then he asked his assistant to take over, removed his mask and washed up. The question was humming in his brain: how on earth could he find four men fit enough to move and travel at night, let alone escape from a seething battle-front bristling with heavy German armour and Panzer units?

'I'm going to alter my normal procedure and make a ward inspection of my lighter cases,' he told the Dutch sister in charge. 'Don't bother to come with me, I only want to see how they're getting along. There's been some talk of cross-infection, and I want to have a look at some of the septic wounds.'

He moved from bed to bed, quietly reading charts. The faces which looked up at him were expectant. Every soldier who'd been in the hospital more than twenty-four hours knew, if only vaguely, that this man was more than an angel of mercy. They waited for news to come from his lips, but this was not his mission now.

Only when he'd completed a tour of the entire post-operative ward did Kessel pause, consult the paper in his hand, and go slowly back to first one, then another, and finally four beds. To each of the occupants he whispered only three words. 'Tonight. Be ready.'

Next day, four empty beds stared blankly at the German nun in charge of administration. It was her job to make a daily check and report on the tally of patients, admissions, deaths, operations, and so on. 'Herr Kessel,' she cried in alarm. 'We have missing four patients!'

Kessel, forced to go through the pretence of accompanying her on her tour, tried to look worried. But his heart raced: they had all made it! Knowing how weak some of the four had been, he had barely slept for worrying about them. Now he knew that at least they had got as far as the 'safe house', and the rest and care of a good Dutch farmer's wife. And, since there had been no hullabaloo in the night, he also knew that no German patrol had spotted their escape.

What could he tell the anxious nun? To gain as much time as possible, Kessel asked to see the ledger. He began a systematic, deliberately muddle-headed check of the figures. Impatience had begun to over-rule civility when a quick-witted young Dutch nurse stepped forward. 'Oh, doctor,' she said to Kessel. 'I have done a dreadful thing! I was so tired last night when I came off duty I quite forgot to report four discharges. A German doctor from the base hospital came while you were asleep in the evening and ordered me to provide four of our lightest cases for orderly duties. The four I let go were all walking-wounded by that time, so I had to agree to him taking them. I'm sorry, doctor, I really should have told you sooner.' And the girl, with a remarkable show of acting talent, burst into tears.

Even the flint-eyed German nun was convinced. Kessel, hiding his relief, quietly dressed down the girl for her carelessness. Then he apologised on her behalf. The nun snapped her book closed. 'So we have four empty beds,' she said. 'Plenty more Britishers will be wounded soon to fill them no doubt!' She would have to wait a long time, Kessel told himself.

As the soldier patients were transferred to P.O.W. camps as soon as they were fit enough to be moved (in spite of Kessel's continuous entreaty that more time was needed for their wounds and operation scars to heal) he turned his thoughts to his own escape. The man who had helped so many others to get away was not going to surrender himself to internment while he had breath in his body.

Lipmann Kessel was another example to me of the value of escape procedures being fully learned and understood by all serving officers before entering combat zones. In his case, the tricks we had instilled into the minds of many of our best and most valuable officers had been well learned. He hid a small button compass in the fly of his trousers, money and a surgical saw in his cap. Telling himself he was ready, but that his first duty was still to the dwindling number of patients under his care, he put off leaving until the last minute. Perhaps the Germans sensed what his intention was.

The order came abruptly one morning, delivered by an officer with a vehicle outside to take him away. Kessel was to go immediately to the Dutch barracks at Apeldoorn, in use as a temporary P.O.W. hospital prior to the prisoners' shipment to Germany. His surgical skills were much needed there, he was told.

How long before he, too, would be sent back with them? He made up his mind during the journey; his getaway had to be soon. At Apeldoorn, on the first suitable night, he cut off the two buttons which, together, made one of my most ingenious compasses (one placed on the other would rotate, laminated dots pointing to the North), used surgical bonesnippers to cut his way through the barbed wire fence round the barracks, and made off down a muddy stream nearby to begin a nightmare journey to the coast. Kessel escaped.

He returned to Europe after the Allied landings had succeeded in driving the Germans from his homeland. Today, he is a respected professor of surgery. I must ask him some time if he kept his fly-button compass, if only as a souvenir of a very gallant operation. The proud memory of it has never left me.

15

FAIR STOOD THE WIND

D-DAY FOR THE French resistance and our agents of the S.O.E. working with them began at 6.30 p.m. on June 5, 1944. At that moment, a message went out over the B.B.C. which had been eagerly awaited: 'It is hot in Suez,' read the announcer in a matter-of-fact tone of voice. No doubt it was, but within twenty-four hours it would be a great deal hotter in the Caen region of Normandy.

How many of my radio sets picked up the fateful words, I can only guess. I know that Guillaume Mercader's radio, hidden in the cellar of his cycle shop, received the message loud and clear. A *Tour de France* champion, this valued resistance leader had been given permission to break the curfew in order to practise his cycling. The Germans hoped by this to improve their image with the French, never realising that Mercader used his 'training runs' to co-ordinate the resistance forces in his area. Equally unknown to them was that the brand new tyres and brake shoes on his cycle were supplied by me, though they were carefully disguised to look well-used.

Now Mercader made a tour of the underground groups. To each of them he said only one word: 'Invasion.' Months of preparation had gone into the plan which was now to be put into effect. 'Plan rouge', as it was called, meant sabotage and destruction on an unprecedented scale. In London we watched anxiously, knowing that if the landings failed these men would have revealed themselves in vain. And yet overall my feeling was one of intense relief. At last, the secret war was coming out into the open.

At 5.50 a.m. next morning, British warships, massed in the Channel, opened fire on targets minutely pinpointed for them by the 'watching eyes' of Intelligence. S.O.E. and the Photographic Reconnaisance Interpretation Units had provided up-to-the-minute pictures. French resistance had sent first reports. Mini-cameras had been clicking away in secret for weeks, building up the most composite survey of the area ever used by an invading force.

A masterpiece of espionage carried out by a French resistance worker provided us with a blue-print of the German's Atlantic Wall defences. This was a bristling fortress of heavy armour hidden inside enormously thick concrete pillboxes and gun emplacements stretching along the French northern Atlantic coast. Knowing the precise thickness of the wall and picking out its camouflaged contours in the Normandy area was crucial to our invasion plan. From the detailed map photographed by this agent we were able to choose the most effective attack method to be used against each sector.

How he did it was a lesson in efficient Intelligence work and a triumph for one of my cameras. The man worked as an interior decorator and the local German commandant, who liked to keep his offices looking immaculate, employed him regularly. Possessed of an abundance of what the French call *monnaie de singe* – in other words, blarney – the decorator had persuaded his employer to let him do overtime at night in order 'to complete the job more quickly.' The rest was easy.

Hidden in his overalls was one of my Minoxes. While alone at night the agent took a series of detailed pictures of every part of the secret blue-print. His film reached London hidden in one of my containers.

M.I.6 then had to decide whether these were the

genuine plans. Could they have been deliberately made 'accessible' to our agent? It seemed quite possible. Indeed, only after the most intensive checking, via S.O.E. and resistance men on the ground, were they grudgingly convinced.

Then, false and genuine airfields had to be checked, a job which our air reconnaisance was unable to do. They were located by agents who contrived to pass by as the sun was setting. If there was no reflected gleam from an aircraft, it would mean that the planes were dummies, made of wood and paper.

Equally, the true thickness of concrete walls and gun-mountings had to be ascertained. Around Calais, where some still remain, the walls were twenty feet thick. Fortunately this was not our first target. The beaches we chose, code-named Juno, Omaha and Utah, lay between Le Havre and Cherbourg. And there the fortifications had been erected in a hurry.

This, and a shortage of cement, led to far less protection for the defenders. Our resistance saboteurs had seen to it in many cases that overmuch sand was used in the mixture. The result was inferior quality unable to stand up to intensive shelling or bombing.

Nevertheless we had to know the exact thickness of the concrete. Only then could the type of armament and explosive needed for its destruction be accurately assessed. An agent would get into conversation with one of the labourers who'd built the place. Most probably they'd meet over a drink in a café. 'Must be half a metre thick, those walls,' the agent would say. The labourer knew very well that they were twice as thick, having had the back-breaking task of pouring the cement for them. Under a little persuasion, his tongue loosened by alcohol, he'd come out with it: 'The Boche leaves nothing to chance,' he'd say. 'Don't you know that? Those walls are at least two metres!'

Oil storage and ammunition dumps had also to be

pin-pointed, so as to be neutralised before D-day. All telephone nerve centres were to be dislocated. The means used to obtain such details as these tended to be either very ingenious or remarkably simple.

For example, a certain blind music teacher was allowed to walk where he chose. The Germans did not bother how near to the fortifications he came. But a very small boy accompanied him on his walks. When the blind teacher asked the boy to explain what he saw, the child would innocently talk about the thick walls being built, the large guns being installed.

This man had a phenomenal memory, and a talent for building up an overall picture of the scene. He had a friend who transcribed his information on to cigarette paper. So, by one means and another, it finally reached our S.O.E. agent, for coded transmission to London.

Again, the mayor of a village near Caen advertised for someone to travel from farm to farm to check on their milk capacity for the benefit of children in the area. One of our agents saw the advertisement and got a friend to apply. The necessary papers for travelling were thereby furnished.

Walking from farm to farm, the agent counted his steps which gave him the approximate distances between fortifications, ack-ack batteries and so on. The sun also caught telltale flashes from the binoculars of Germans watching the movements of civilians. Thus he knew which areas to avoid and where it was too dangerous to make notes.

In these parts, while smoking he would bite his match-stick: a quarter mark meant 25 metres; a half match, 50 metres; and a whole match 100 metres. Later, he constructed the fortifications' layout, from these indentations.

Another ingenious method for secretly marking distances was used by a woman agent who travelled as a bona-fide farmer's wife on buses crammed with passengers, geese and sacks of potatoes. Always resting on her knee was a knitting book. From time to time she would note numbers of rows and stitches in it, as she knitted. These, had anybody realised it, represented new roads, distances between them, or new tracks and ways made to the cliffs; and so on.

But perhaps the most ingenious deception of all was the way in which the Germans were persuaded that the attacks on Omaha and neighbouring beaches were only a feint. As a result, the mass of German armour was held back in the Pas de Calais area awaiting the major thrust there. It was some days before the Germans realised their mistake. By then the Normandy beachhead had been established. One of my last contributions to the landings had been to provide proper waterproofing for the amphibious tanks that were to be used. I managed it by supplying special adhesives developed from those used in our radium sphere landing lights. Not one of the tanks suffered any leakage to its vital parts.

Though this moment was very much the climax of our secret war the need for total secrecy was even greater than before. The strength of our security at this time explained why so little of our invasion plans reached Hitler or his generals.

The night before D-day, hand-picked officers were ordered to leave their units for special duty. Separately each one was driven on a random course through the English countryside. Transferred from one staff car to another, they were at last brought to the nerve-centre controlling the entire invasion. Each officer was then handed a sealed package containing detailed orders for a specific unit.

'Take these,' he was told, 'to the officer commanding...' A code-name for a particular unit followed. No destination. No details, but a grim rider: 'Demand the password. If he doesn't give it, shoot him dead. Then return these to me.'

The officers were then escorted away. Each spent the night in a special, wired-off security area, completely alone. Patrolling sentries carried live grenades. The pin had been removed so that only hand pressure kept the bomb from exploding, thus dramatically preventing sleep.

In the early dawn, the officers were returned to their transports to be driven on another long, confusing route. Ultimately, each was brought face to face with the commander of a spearhead detachment to request the vital password.

The story, I think, demonstrates how security had improved as a result of experience. We had suspected at Dieppe and during the bitter Norwegian campaigns, that our security had been inadequate. The way these D-day orders were delivered was an indication that, whatever else, we had learnt a major lesson in the long war years. Secrecy cannot be overdone in a fight with a clever, ruthless enemy.

Now, in June 1944, we were at last on the offensive in Western Europe, but the war in Europe was far from won. D-day's landings gave us a precarious toe-hold, no more. When our forces eventually broke out of the Caen beachheads they faced a long, hard slog to reach Germany's heart.

My own work, too, continued at full stretch, supplying evasion kits to the increasing numbers of airmen now operating over Europe, as well as providing supplies and equipment to the still highly active agents of the S.O.E. and various underground organisations.

In my view no praise can be too high for these secret warriors. The number of Allied lives saved by the keen eyes of the resistance on D-day alone is incalculable, though in the invasion sector more than 2,500 decorations and awards for valour were made to civilians.

Day after day these men and women continued against

the greatest odds and with no-one present to encourage them. Seldom was it possible to let them know if their arduous and perilous work was successful. Much of it went unrecognised. Those who fought in the Services were spurred on by team spirit, *ésprit de corps.* The S.O.E. agent and the resistance fighter were alone. This was the highest order of heroism.

Indeed, it was the true backbone and sinew of our ultimate success. Hidden behind every great event in the war were these heroes and heroines, unknown, and unsung for the most part, since no war correspondents shared their isolated theatres. They gave the generals and war leaders the information which made the latter famous. Yet in many cases no credit or acknowledgement was made.

With the major exceptions of Churchill and Eisenhower, few of the victorious generals and others who wrote of their campaigns in World War Two even mentioned them. I dedicate this book as much to them as to my many selfless suppliers already mentioned.

In today's Special Air Services we have an example of how small forces, used in carefully planned strategic operations, can play a decisive role against cumbersome regular war machines. It reminds me of the many gadgets, and other material, I supplied to David Stirling and his men of the S.A.S. from the time of its inauguration in North Africa.

Stirling's name is among those in my little note-book, as is that of Dare Newell, who formed one of the most daring of the early S.A.S. groups operating in the long-range desert warfare campaign. I thought of him, too, when the success of the S.A.S. in the Iranian Embassy Siege in London in 1980 showed the world what they could do, using personal and individual courage and resourcefulness and carefully selected equipment. The question it brought to my mind was whether we still continue to maintain the many materials and gadgets perfected in wartime.

Such a 'storehouse' could prove invaluable for the secret equipping of future 'Q' forces. In World War Two it took many months to organise S.O.E. into a reasonably effective unit. Time needed for such organisation cost lives, and remembering how hopelessly adrift I was in an uncharted sea during the early days of my specific 'Q' operations, I would urge with all my heart the maintainance of at least the basic requirements. I believe there could be no better investment our country could make by way of preparation to meet aggression.

So far, nuclear weapons have saved us, and given us the longest period of peace in Europe for a century or more. How much longer they will do so, nobody can say. From the time when Tube Alloys would ring me for the best and most reliable secret contacts at the firms I was dealing with (and, as I later learnt, used them for work on the first atomic bomb), I have supported the use of this terrible weapon at Hiroshima and Nagasaki. In my opinion, only the short-sighted disclaim this act which saved not only Allied but also Japanese lives. We were fighting a fanatical enemy who showed that he preferred to fight to the death rather than surrender. To capture Okinawa, the Americans lost 50,000 men, but the Japanese held on until every one of their 100,000 was killed. If they defended an outpost like that, would they have done less for their homeland?

Yet the question I also ask myself in the quiet and peace of my home on the edge of Exmoor is whether we rely too much on the nuclear shield. Readiness, I believe, is the only way to stop a Third World War, and not only in the nuclear field.

Finally, there is the moral question. Is secret warfare, with all its many deceits and subterfuges, to be condoned? Does my conscience accept the necessity for the many tricks and devices I developed? Emphatically yes.

Secret Intelligence and secret agents such as the

S.O.E. are as old as the hills. We have examples in the Bible such as the capture of Jericho in 1451 BC. Even the New Testament teaches the absolute necessity of being armed to the teeth for just defence. To quote Jesus Christ: 'When a strong man, *fully armed,* guards his own place, his possessions are safe.'

There are, of course, both spiritual and physical forms of armament. To wage the secret warfare of my 'Q' operations, faith was an essential element. I recall how a great and heroic Frenchman, André Dewavrin, who under the code name Colonel Passey helped establish the underground network of Intelligence and resistance in France, replied to anyone paying tribute to his personal vision and courage. 'No, no, it is of the others you have to talk and write about, because they had the *faith.*' Very much like the Bible, you know – what Paul said in the Book to the Hebrews. He talks about men like Noah, Abraham and others, and he says "faith is the substance of things hoped for, the evidence of things not seen". A modern translation from the Greek expresses it more clearly: "To have faith is to be sure of the things we hope for and to be certain of the things we cannot see." '

So this is my answer. I would add, for myself and for the men and women who made the 'Q tricks', those words of the Psalmist: 'Blessed be God who trains my hands and fingers for warfare.' He did just this in World War Two.

INDEX